KNIGHTMARE CAPITAL

EDWARD W. PAGE

Dedication

To my parents, for the wonderful life you gave me, the moral compass that has guided me, for the gift of dreams, and the courage to chase them.

Contents

Dedication III

Author's Note V

Prologue VI

Chapter One: Meet and Greet 1

Chapter Two: A New Beginning 13

Chapter Three: Getting Into The Business 27

Chapter Four: Going into Hyperdrive 41

Chapter Five: Arrival at the Peak 56

Chapter Six: The Slide 67

Chapter Seven: Gone Fishing 85

Chapter Eight: Game-Changing 95

Chapter Nine: What Now? 109

Chapter Ten: Meet Me in St. Louis 120

Chapter Eleven: Moving on Along 131

Chapter Twelve: Taking Off the Gloves 142

Chapter Thirteen: Another Hit 160

Chapter Fourteen: Heat in the Kitchen 173

Chapter Fifteen: Sweet Fifteen 183

Epilogue 193

Author's Note

More than 20 years after these events took place, I began writing about them. What started out as a therapeutic exercise slowly evolved, over the course of 12 years, into this book. Never in a million years did I imagine that I would write one, but as the story took shape, I realized that it needed to be told.

At its core, this is a story about not wavering on principles when it would be easier, and perhaps more profitable, to discard them. It's about choosing what's right, no matter the cost. While the book primarily revolves around business, the values it reflects apply to everything in life.

I hope this story provides inspiration to everyone going through difficult times, whether in their personal life or their career. Integrity may not always be the easiest path, but in the end, it's always the one worth taking.

Prologue

"Oh, Ed! You should write a book—no, you must write one! Your life is an absolute rollercoaster. You really should share your story. Give the people what they want—nay—need!"

Those words were practically shouted at me every single time I told anyone the short, sanitized version of what happened all those years ago. It happened so often that the time finally came for me to write this story.

I initially never thought much of it—the story, I mean. It was my life, my work, my chaos. But to others, it sounded completely fabricated. Whenever I told it to anyone, disbelief was the common reaction. It sounded too wild, too far-fetched to be true. But I lived it.

It all began when I landed one of the most exhilarating jobs I could have ever imagined in the dynamic, fast-paced world of private equity in New York City. It was a leap of faith since I had just switched over from the steady, predictable, and mind-numbing world of surety bond underwriting and commercial banking. Seven years of buttoned-up suits, nine-to-five schedules, and calculated, measured risks had left me feeling...*restless.* When the management at my bank changed, bringing in a senior lender who seemed more focused on closing doors than opening them, I knew it was time to move on. Add to that the disastrous and sudden collapse of my first marriage, and I found myself craving something new—something *thrilling.*

Everyone urged me to stick to the conventional path, the one that was 'safe' and predictable. But I had outgrown the need for safety.

I tossed everything aside and left it all behind to join a fledgling firm that had one operating company and eight employees at headquarters. It was a risky move, but I was young and fearless, with nothing to lose. The chairman, a charismatic genius with a taste for the finer things in life, showed me the ropes. The day I met him, he told me he saw something in me. At the time, I took it as a compliment. Later, however, I'd wonder if it was something else entirely.

From day one, I quickly learned that this job was more than I had ever imagined. I was signing up for a new and improved lifestyle. Before I knew it, I was on planes more often than I was on solid ground, flitting around North America and Europe most of the year. My actual home back in St. Louis became little more than a place to collect mail.

The chairman of Kenmare Capital had a mantra he'd often chant to us: "If commercial banks are open, *we are open*." And we were. Day trips to Atlanta, Chicago, and Dallas on the Friday after Thanksgiving? Routine. A last-minute flight to London to meet with a banker? Just another Tuesday.

The pace almost got too much to keep up with, and it was always a race against the clock. But here's the funny part: I thrived on it. I was surrounded by brilliance—financial experts, engineering masterminds, and a network of lawyers, accountants, and investment bankers who knew everything about everything. They taught me, shaped me, and sharpened me. Within a year, I was closing deals on my own, acquisitions that turned out to be some of the most profitable in the firm's history: Kolpak Refrigeration and Detroit Tool. Each one a feather in my hat, each one moving me one step closer to becoming indispensable.

But the chairman had a way of blurring the lines between work and play. Business dinners would often turn into late-night parties. Deals were sealed over whiskey and cigars, sometimes in private rooms with music so loud you could feel it thump in your chest. There were nights I don't remember, and some mornings I'd rather forget. The Chairman's taste for excess was infectious. Escorts, champagne showers, body shots—nights bled into the sunrise in the blink of an eye and left you with nothing but a throbbing headache and a fuzzy memory—it was all part of the package.

And then there was that September morning.

That crisp autumn morning wasn't just a date on the calendar. It was a line in the sand. I had woken up groggy, my head pounding from the previous night's indulgences. It was the kind of haze that comes from too many gin and tonics and Chardonnays, not enough sleep. The bedside phone rang incessantly on the nightstand, each time cutting through the fog in my head. When I finally answered, the voice on the other end was sharp, devoid of pleasantries. "Get to the office. Now."

I sat there for a moment, staring at the sunlight filtering through the blinds, trying to gather my thoughts, strewn all over the place like my clothes on the floor. The events of the previous night flickered like a reel on fast-forward—booze, smoke, people conversing animatedly and passing around a rolled-up hundred dollars to others who wished to partake, and a woman whose face was already fading from memory. None of it mattered now.

I lit a cigarette, the first drag settling my nerves as I tried to piece together what was coming. The urgency in that voice told me everything I needed to know: this wasn't just another day. I dressed quickly, the suit feeling heavier than usual as I pulled it on. By the time I stepped out the door, I knew a storm was already brewing. I still managed to make it to the office early, my New York regular coffee steaming in my hand, already knee-deep in a second call before most people had even started their commute.

Then the Chairman waltzed in. On that particular morning, he wasn't quite himself. The usual bravado, the larger-than-life presence that entered the room before he did, was absent. There was something off-base; I could feel it in my bones. He closed the door behind him, something he rarely ever did, and I felt the air shift. "We have a problem," he told me.

What followed wasn't a conversation. It was a gut punch. A moment where everything I thought I knew began to fall apart at the seams. I can't tell you exactly what he said—not yet. But I can tell you this: it was the moment I realized the man I'd admired, the one I thought I owed everything to, wasn't who he appeared to be.

In the days that followed, the atmosphere in the office was nothing less than suffocating. Chatter turned to murmurs. Closed-door meetings became the norm.

Documents appeared and disappeared like ghosts. And slowly, painfully, I began to piece together a truth I wasn't prepared for in the slightest. The chairman had made moves—calculated, ruthless moves—that jeopardized not just the company, but the livelihoods of everyone tied to it, including me. It wasn't just business; it was war. Gradually, a picture began to emerge, one that I wished I could unsee. It wasn't just a corporate misstep; it was a betrayal, one that would ripple far beyond the conference room.

Over the years, I had learned everything there was to know about the game: spotting opportunities, making deals, structuring them, running companies, and, when necessary, tearing them apart. I didn't just grow in the job—I became a weapon. My contributions to the firm were undeniable, and the chairman seemed pleased to have me in his corner. Everything I had worked for at the firm became my arsenal when everything fell apart after that morning.

I had to look up the old proverb, "Everything good must come to an end." Turns out, the saying actually goes like this: "There is an end to everything and good things as well," from Chaucer, way back in 1374. Either way, the sentiment hit home. That September morning was more than a beginning. It was the moment the ground shifted beneath me, the first move in a game that would change everything. This is the story of me, Edward W. Page, and my journey through the meteoric rise and catastrophic fall of Kenmare Capital Corp.

Chapter One: Meet and Greet

Every so often, someone steps into your life and, without you even realizing it, completely flips the script. A chance meeting, a handshake, or a passing introduction can set you on a path you never saw coming. For me, that someone was Daniel J. Sullivan—a connection made almost by fluke.

The year was 1983, and I was grinding it out as a commercial lender at Mark Twain Banks in St. Louis, Missouri. Banking was steady and relatively stable work, and St. Louis had its own charm—a city with just enough hustle to keep things interesting. That's when I met good old Dan, and my world started to shift.

Dan was more than your run-of-the-mill client. He had that rare combination of charisma and mystery, the kind of guy who could hold court in a boardroom or a bar with equal ease. He was tall, sharp, and carried himself with the confidence of someone who knew the game and, most importantly, how to win it. Dan was in partnership with Stephen L. Trampe, a sharp, light-haired St. Louis native who was making waves in the high-end real estate market in St. Louis and was a customer at the bank.

Steve had deep connections to the real estate, art, and music scenes in the region. The Central West End, a hip and trendy area of St. Louis, was his canvas, and he painted it with sleek, first-class condo developments that sold faster than a bartender could pour a drink. The buildings he developed weren't just regular condos—they were high-end, thoughtfully designed spaces that quickly became some of the most sought-after locations in the city. The sell-through rates were impressive, and the bank took pride in being the lender he trusted to bring these projects to life. Each of Steve's projects stood as a bold statement.

Dan, though, had a bigger story. Real estate was just one slice of his pie. His main game was leveraged buyouts, a world I'd only heard about in passing. His forte was acquiring underperforming companies across North America and Europe, slapping them with a shiny new management team, usually a new president and chief financial officer, and turning them into profit-churning machines by the dozen. It was the kind of high-stakes, high-reward business that came with whiskey-fueled celebrations and the occasional shattered glass.

Dan's deals were truly the stuff of legend; big debt, bigger risk, and a certain swagger that screamed, '*We've got this.*'. He had a knack for spotting potential in what others had written off. His process was surgical: buy low, fix fast, and sell high. Key players were swapped out like overplayed records, and new strategies were hammered into place during marathon due diligence sessions. By the time the ink dried on the acquisition documents, Dan's team would have already mapped out how to turn the ship around.

After spending a lot of time with Dan in both St. Louis and New York, I was mesmerized by the scale of his operations and found them endlessly fascinating. His world was bold, fast-paced, and just risky enough to keep things exciting. That intrigue led Mark Twain Bank to dive deeper into his orbit, moving beyond local real estate deals into something far bigger. We took a major leap, refinancing high-yield leveraged buyout loans for one of Dan's commercial food service equipment manufacturing groups.

Mark Twain, a regional bank not exactly known for swinging far and wide, geographically, really stepped up with Dan and his company, Bastian International Holdings, Inc. The collateral backing these loans wasn't your standard fare. Rather, it was a cluster of industrial manufacturing facilities scattered across the United States—St. Louis, Washington, Missouri; Grand Haven, Michigan; and Philadelphia, Pennsylvania. It was a gamble, but one with a serious upside.

At 2 ¾ points over prime on several million dollars, the yields on these loans were unlike anything I'd witnessed before; they were ridiculously spectacular. The bank was raking in fat margins, and I was right in the middle of it all, watching as this partnership turned into a high-stakes banking game. It was what made my spirit soar, and proof that stepping out of one's comfort zone could pay off big time.

Spending time with Dan soon became more than just business. Our professional relationship deepened, and so did our personal connection. He had a sprawling red-brick mansion on Portland Place in St. Louis, 12,000 square feet to be exact, where he hosted black-tie New Year's Eve parties, which were something else. The house itself was a statement—red brick, towering windows, and an interior that screamed old money with a modern twist. Those parties would have made even Gatsby's guests bow their heads in shame. The guest list consisted of the elite of St. Louis and

New York; throw a few wild cards in the mix, and you've added just the right amount of unpredictability. There was always a live band, an open bar stocked with top-shelf everything, and enough whiskey to drown a small army. Conversations flowed as freely as the drinks, and deals were sometimes sketched out on cocktail napkins between bites of caviar.

Then there was his New York Brownstone, sleek and understated, but its energy was pure Manhattan. I remember walking through it, feeling like I had stepped into a dream. Those nights in New York were a different kind of education. Dinners turned into strategy sessions, which turned into wild debates over who could spot the next big opportunity. The drinks flowed, the cigars burned long, and the stories got louder as the night went on. It wasn't unusual for someone to pull out a bottle of something rare and expensive, just to see if it could top what we'd already had.

Dan, in his mid-40s, was the epitome of cool. At 6'4", with a streak of gray in his hair and those round horn-rimmed glasses he'd remove when reading, he looked every bit the part of the sophisticated businessman. But what set him apart was his exceptional ability to juggle the pressures of his work while maintaining a strong, loving presence in his family's life.

See, Dan had an unusually dual life: family man in St. Louis and corporate shark in Manhattan. He had a wife and five kids in St. Louis, where life seemed almost idyllic, yet he somehow managed a corporate empire out of Manhattan, where the pace was relentless. It was a life that seemed both grounded and glamorous—a rare combination.

He once told me that St. Louis had a special place in his heart. Early in his career, he worked in corporate development at Monsanto's headquarters. When it came time to settle down and start a family, he remembered St. Louis as the perfect place to do it. "You can live like a king here," he said one night over a drink, "and still play with the sharks in New York." He made it look effortless, like balancing two lives was just another skill he'd mastered.

Spending time with Dan in both St. Louis and New York was like living in two different worlds, each with its own rhythm and rhyme. The more I got to know him and his operations, the more fascinated I became. Dan had this uncanny ability to blend the grit of high-stakes business with the charm of an effortless host. It wasn't just about the deals; it was about the lifestyle, the connections, and the sheer audacity of it all.

For me, coming from the grind of banking, Dan's world seemed intoxicating. St. Louis had its charm, but New York was electric. The deals, the pace, the people—it was all bigger, faster, and right up my alley. Dan and I shared a respect for both cities. St. Louis was where you built a home; New York was where you made a name.

To think all of this happened a thousand miles west of my original East Coast stomping grounds is truly amazing. After graduating from St. Michael's College in Vermont with a degree in economics, I started my professional journey as a surety bond underwriter with The Chubb Group of Insurance Companies in Short Hills, New Jersey. It was a serious gig—essentially, we were the safety net for construction projects. If a contractor botched the job or couldn't pay their subs, the bonds we issued guaranteed the project would still get done, and everyone would get paid. It was all about evaluating risk, digging into financials, and making judgment calls on whether a company had the chops to deliver.

Two years in, Chubb transferred me to their branch office in Clayton, Missouri, a swanky suburb of St. Louis. The move was a breath of fresh air. St. Louis had a slower pace than New Jersey, and the cost of living meant I could actually afford to enjoy myself. Plus, the skills I'd honed in underwriting translated seamlessly when I jumped ship to Mark Twain Banks. Commercial lending wasn't just a job; it was a front-row seat to the inner workings of countless industries. Every loan was a story, and every borrower was a character.

At Mark Twain, the atmosphere was lively, and I made many lasting friendships there. Unlike Chubb's small, buttoned-up office in Clayton, the bank was expansive, with hundreds of employees and plenty of ambitious twenty- and thirty-somethings looking to make their mark, just like me.

As a commercial lender, I gained direct exposure to a whole world of businesses and industries that went way beyond just contracting. The job was like a backstage pass to a wide range of career options, opening doors to all sorts of ventures and opportunities. But as the days went by, I couldn't shake the pull of Dan's work: acquiring and managing groups of manufacturing companies. It was gritty, it was complex, and it had a raw potential that grasped me more and more with every passing day.

Despite my growing fascination with Dan's operations, my career up to that point had already been shaped by my foundational experiences in surety bond underwriting and commercial lending. Those early years taught me how to evaluate credit and operational risks with a sharp eye—skills that would later become invaluable. But life has a way of throwing curveballs when you least expect them, and my carefully planned trajectory was about to take a wild turn when life threw a grenade into the mix.

My wife of five years decided to have an affair with her boss at work. I came home one evening to find a goodbye note on the dinner table; talk about a clichéd way to end a marriage. She cleaned out the house, loaded up her car with everything that would fit, and returned to the New York metropolitan area and moved in with her parents. From what I heard later, her boss went home that same night to his wife and three kids. The family promptly packed their bags and moved to Connecticut to avoid embarrassment. It was a scandal that had tongues wagging for weeks.

For me, though, it was a wake-up call. The dissolution of my marriage forced me to reevaluate everything—my career, my priorities, and what I wanted out of life. Nights that were once spent schmoozing clients turned into long, introspective evenings with gin and tonics, Chardonnays, and a playlist of classic rock peppered with occasional heartbreak ballads. I wasn't just thinking about the end of my marriage; I was grappling with a sense of discontent.

Dan, in my moments of contemplating what to do next, became a mentor, a friend, and, in many ways, a guide into a world I hadn't known existed. Banking had been good to me, but it wasn't enough anymore. Even with all its perks, it began to feel hollow. I wanted in on the action, the thrill, and the chance to build something bigger than just a loan portfolio. Dan saw it too.

Over the course of that year, as I wrestled with my thoughts about the future, Dan left his cushy investment group to form his own firm. It was bold, reckless even, but it was pure Dan. Far be it from him to casually dip his toes into uncharted waters—he cannonballed in, making waves and taking names.

What started as casual chats about leveraged buyouts and strategic plans evolved into serious conversations about me leaving the bank and joining his newly formed venture. Dan, a master at spotting potential, saw something in me I hadn't yet recognized in myself.

But he didn't sugarcoat it for me either. "Once you leave the conventional world," he warned, "you can't go back." It was a line that stuck with me, even as the allure of his world pulled me closer. This wasn't just a job change; it was a leap into the unknown, where the stakes were higher, the risks were graver, and the safety nets non-existent. But even with that ominous disclaimer, our conversations kept going. The more we talked, the more I felt like I was standing on the edge of a cliff, staring down at a world that was both terrifying and invigorating.

It wasn't just about escaping the bank or the shadow of my failed marriage. It was about stepping into a world that felt bigger, bolder, and full of possibility. And with Dan at the helm, I knew the ride would be anything but ordinary.

By the time June 1985 rolled around, I took the plunge. I was done sitting on the sidelines. Banking had started to feel like a suit that didn't fit anymore. Sure, it was comfortable, but it was also stifling. I wanted something more, something with teeth. I left the safe confines of regional banking and stepped into the high-stakes world of private equity. So, I joined Dan's fledgling firm as a vice president. It didn't even have its final name yet—it would soon become Kenmare Capital Corp.

The office was a far cry from the buttoned-up world of regional banking. Deals were hashed out over long dinners that blurred into after-hours bar crawls. The lines between work and play didn't just blur; they disappeared entirely. One night, we'd be celebrating a new acquisition with top-shelf whiskey and Cuban cigars; the next, we'd be back at it, poring over spreadsheets and arguing strategy until dawn. It was messy, chaotic, and utterly addictive.

Dan wasn't wrong about the point of no return. Once you stepped into this world, there was no going back to a conventional office setting. But for the first time in a long time, I felt alive. This was more than just a career move for me. It was a reinvention.

It was a move that would change everything, and I had Dan Sullivan to thank for it. I knew I was stepping into a life that was as unpredictable as it was electrifying. It was so much more than the money or the deals. It was about the people, the moments, and the sheer ecstasy of the ride. And to think, it all started with a handshake in St. Louis.

Chapter Two: A New Beginning

The jump from commercial lending to private equity, later spun into something flashier by the leveraged buyout crowd, was a big adjustment for me. The career shift came with a whole new way of thinking. No more sitting back, evaluating risk from a safe, comfortable distance. Now, I was in the thick of it, making the plays instead of just observing and assessing them. The first thing I had on my radar was to ditch the old banker mindset and start thinking from the perspective of a principal as opposed to a creditor.

Then came the daunting task of learning my way around a Compaq portable computer—an absolute brick of a machine—and the Lotus 123 software. That beast of a computer got dragged across North America and Europe, and from New York to the Midwest. I had to split my time between St. Louis and Dan Sullivan's slick new office on the 20th floor of the Metropolitan Life Insurance Building in Manhattan. That place was something else, with dark wood columns, brass fixtures, and white marble floors. It screamed wealth, affluence, and a little bit of well-earned arrogance.

Dan's team consisted of shrewd minds and seasoned pros who knew how to close a deal and celebrate it in equal measure. The roster:

- Gilbert Raker, Executive Vice President
- John Sullivan, Senior Vice President
- William Laverty, Director of Acquisitions
- Andrew Mayer, Controller

To say that these people were good with numbers was an understatement; they were dealmakers, hustlers, and, when the work was done (or even when it wasn't), experts in finding the best bars and restaurants in Manhattan.

At the time, there was only one other company that generated management fees—the recurring payments from operating companies to private equity firms, covering salaries, travel, rent, utilities, and other operational costs. It was called CPC Industries, a sprawling commercial and industrial painting contractor that raked in around $25 million a year, with facilities in St. Louis, Chicago, Salt Lake City, and Concord, California. A messy, far-flung operation. And the best part? Dan bought it with zero money down. He handed over CPC's own cash, threw in a note secured by the St. Louis assets, and walked away with the keys. Just like that, he owned the company, a straightforward and effortless purchase.

But there was a dent in the plan: CPC wasn't a manufacturer, which made it an oddball acquisition for Dan. Along with handing over the cash and the note to the seller in satisfaction of the agreed purchase price, Dan also secured a line of credit from Mark Twain to fund future operations. Despite having little experience in the commercial and industrial contracting industry, he couldn't resist the opportunity.

Thanks to Dan and the New York crew, our group had an almost endless stream of deals coming our way. Investment banks, business brokers, and well-connected insiders constantly pitched us companies for sale. This 'deal flow' was everything. Without it, we were just burning through CPC's management fees, and CPC alone wasn't enough to keep the lights on forever. It was a race against time to find another company to acquire or risk running out of cash.

We needed a real acquisition, something big, something fast. And in 1986, we caught a big fish: Pangborn

Corporation, a $50 million industrial manufacturer of blast cleaning and surface preparation equipment, with operations in the United States, Canada, the United Kingdom, and Italy. We bought it from Standard Oil Company of Ohio for $30 million—a steal. And just in time. CPC had managed to keep its head above water long enough not to screw up the deal.

The moment that the deal closed, CPC became dead weight. My job, along with John Sullivan's, was to chop it up, sell off the pieces, and make sure no one got left holding the bag. Funnily enough, John, Dan's younger brother, was notoriously known as 'the bag man'; whenever there was an unpleasant task to handle for Dan, John was the one who got the call. If something needed to get done but was too messy, too tedious, or too dicey for Dan to touch, John handled it. He was Dan's right-hand man, the one who handled the dirty work. If there was a mess, John was the guy sent in to clean it up.

I first met John when I was still on the other side of the table, negotiating CPC's financing. He had been Dan's frontman in those discussions, and I quickly learned that he had an unnatural level of patience. He could sit through hours of negotiations without breaking a sweat, calmly wearing down the other side until they gave in just to get out of the room. He had a way of making silence uncomfortable, letting it stretch on to an unsettling degree until the person across from him started talking just to fill the void. That's when he'd strike.

John was tall like Dan, but leaner, with brown hair just beginning to show streaks of grey. He lived in Dobbs Ferry, New York, with his wife and kids, commuting into the city daily, a long-winded three-hour round trip that would have driven most people insane. But John took it in stride, just like he did everything else. He never complained or lost his cool. He was relatively satisfied with his situation at work.

Although when CPC fell into our lap, keeping it afloat was no easy feat. We were constantly scrambling for cash, smoothing over problems, and making sure the operation didn't collapse before we could land our next deal. The stress was high, but so were the rewards. Late nights in the office turned into late nights at the bar, where we drowned our exhaustion in expensive alcohol. Deals were made over steak dinners and sealed with too many drinks at places where the lights were low and the tabs were high.

By the time Pangborn was officially ours, CPC had served its purpose. It had bought us time, kept the machine running, and given John and me a crash course in survival. Pangborn had finally come through, replacing CPC as our primary cash generator. That meant one thing: it was time to put CPC out of its misery. The writing had been on the wall for a while; none of us had any business running a commercial contracting company. We were Irish Catholic finance guys from New York, not construction bosses. It was time to cut our losses and get the hell out.

John and I spent most of 1986 dismantling CPC, piece by piece. We sold off the Salt Lake City and Concord operations to their respective division presidents, handed the St. Louis assets back to the former owner, and sold the Chicago facility to a private investor group. The Mark Twain Bank line of credit was repaid, and just like that, we were out of the business for good.

Of course, it wasn't as easy as just walking away. There were bonds to unwind, contracts to close, and a whole lot of creative problem-solving required to make it all work. My past experience with Chubb turned out to be invaluable. We had to dissect CPC's backlog, breaking down overbilling, underbilling, and remaining gross margins to package them up for sale or subcontracting. It was like playing a high-stakes game of financial Jenga, hoping the whole thing wouldn't collapse before we cashed out.

Then there was the California problem. A non-union subsidiary was sitting in a pristine, leased office warehouse near Concord, but there were no buyers. The lease had a couple of years left, and we weren't about to eat that cost. So, in the dead of night, over a single weekend, we cleared the place out. Every piece of inventory, every scrap of equipment, every truck and tool—we moved it all, adding it to the Concord sale. When we locked up, John had one final order: "Make sure it's broom-swept, clean as a whistle."

John always believed bad news went down easier when it was wrapped in a pretty package. So, we left the keys in plain sight, wiped our fingerprints off the doorknobs, and walked away. CPC was history, and we were finally free to focus on bigger and better things.

Some of the negotiations for the sale of CPC's Concord, California, operation took place in New York City. On one of those trips, the President of the division handled our hotel arrangements—four nights for him, three for me. Not exactly the most frugal guy, he booked us at none other than The Plaza Hotel, one of Manhattan's most iconic and lavish addresses.

He flew in from California a day before me. I went straight from LaGuardia to his attorney's office in Midtown for a full day of negotiations. That session went well into the night, and I didn't arrive at The Plaza until about 1:30 a.m. the next morning.

At check-in, the front desk attendant looked surprised. Apparently, they had assumed I was a no-show and gave away my room. After disappearing into a back office to speak with a supervisor, he returned and informed me—very apologetically—that they'd be upgrading me to a suite for the same rate. No extra charge.

The bellman escorted me upstairs, opened the door, and I just stood there. My jaw practically hit the floor. This suite was fit for royalty—sprawling living area, two bedrooms, two marble bathrooms, and furnishings straight out of a luxury design magazine.

All I could think was: *This is it. When I wrap up tomorrow's negotiations, I'm calling up my friends in the city. We're going to party like rock stars right here at The Plaza.*

But of course, the next day's session went long again. Excruciatingly long. We wrapped up late into the night—too late for calls, plans, or parties. Still, I had one night left. One final shot at making that suite count. Then it happened again. Another marathon session, another midnight finish. By the time I got back to the hotel, I was too tired to care. I had maybe logged a total of 18 hours in the suite, most of it asleep. No friends, no party, no wild night at The Plaza. Looking back, it's probably for the best. We would've trashed the place anyway.

Back in St. Louis, while shutting down the CPC operation, I stumbled upon one of the more bizarre employee arrangements I'd ever seen. There was a guy on the payroll who collected two separate paychecks, one that he sent to an Illinois address just across the river and the other that was addressed to a town in Missouri about 40 miles south. Turns out, he had two families, living two separate lives, completely unaware of each other. When I let him go, he was livid, as if I had taken the time to personally torpedo his master plan. I had to wonder how he'd manage to pull that off with his next employer.

The St. Louis division itself was hemorrhaging money, mostly due to bad job estimates and botched execution. The Union Station renovation project was a prime example. Painting the historic train shed should have been straightforward, but our "skilled" laborers managed to coat over 500 passing vehicles on Highway 40 with a fine mist of overspray. The job had been completed, but the mess it left behind was a headache and a half. With no one else in the office, I found myself playing middleman between irate car owners and the South St. Louis body shops contracted by the insurance company to mitigate the damage.

Watching those guys work was a sight to behold. They'd lather each car in soap, then use thin, double-edged razor blades—barehanded—to scrape the microscopic paint particles off every surface.

One afternoon, I returned a pickup truck to Enterprise Rental's St. Louis headquarters, where I met Ernie, the guy in charge of finance and leasing. He was genuinely shocked that I had taken the time to return the truck myself and even more impressed that it was spotless. “Nobody does this,” he said, shaking his head. “I’m so grateful.” I nodded, remembering John’s mantra about taking responsibility and going the extra mile.

Then I asked if I could use his phone. As I hung up, Ernie raised an eyebrow. “Something I can help you with?”

“No,” I replied, looking down at my watch. “But in about fifteen minutes, you’re going to have eight more pickups just like this one rolling in.”

Dan’s oldest son and his buddies were already stationed at the office, waiting for my call. They’d scrubbed down every truck, inside and out, making sure they were pristine. It was a final and clean break from CPC. As I walked out of Enterprise, I felt a strange feeling of satisfaction. We had dismantled an entire operation, sold off what we could, and tied up the loose ends without leaving a complete disaster in our wake.

That night, I met John for a drink. We raised our glasses, toasting to the chaos we had just survived without so much as a scratch. “Never again,” he said. I laughed and replied, “Never say never.”

Thanks to my time with CPC, I became something of a specialist in handing out pink slips—as ghoulish as that sounds. By sometime later in 1986, that particular skill set led to an unusual assignment. Dan still had an ownership stake in a scrap yard in Dayton, Ohio, a remnant from a past investment partnership that was now circling the drain. The place was shutting down, and they needed someone with zero ties to the operation to deliver the final blow. An outsider. Anonymous. No fingerprints. That's where I came in.

Even the limo driver wasn't given my real name. That alone should have been my first clue that this wasn't just another routine termination. But the real warning came when they casually mentioned the guy I was firing had managed to beat a double murder charge on a technicality. And yet, that wasn't even my biggest worry. No, the real danger, they said, was his wife—meaner than a two-headed snake and twice as unpredictable. The kind of woman who wouldn't just take revenge. No, she'd make it personal.

So, I flew into Dayton under the radar, got picked up in the pre-arranged limo, and was dropped off just down the street from the yard. No grand entrances. No unnecessary conversations. Just business. I walked into the drab, grease-stained office, collected the final paycheck, and made my way out to the yard where the man in question was operating a crane.

He was massive, built like a wrecking ball. But his movements were slower than what I would have anticipated. *"Alright, maybe I can outrun him if things go south,"* I thought.

I called out to him, asked for a moment, and as he climbed down, I handed him the check. I kept it short, didn't reveal my real name, and went in, unsure of how it would unfold.

"The company's shutting down. This is your final pay, through the end of the day."

He looked at me blankly, and all he said was, "Okay."

That was it. No questions. No pushback.

I walked with him as he gathered a few personal items from the office, and just like that, he was gone. I didn't wait around to see if his wife came storming in, ready to rip someone's head off. I hailed the limo, and within minutes, I was on my way back to New York. The entire job took less than five hours, but I'd be lying if I said I didn't wonder about the aftermath; I can only imagine the conversation when he got home.

"Who fired you?"

"Dunno. Some guy in a suit. Never seen him before."

I bet she gave him hell for it anyway. But as far as I know, that was the end of it: no fallout and no retaliation. Just another day in the business of making things disappear.

And so, with CPC on its way to the scrapyard and Pangborn humming along as a steady cash machine, it was time to build something new. In April 1986, Kenmare Capital Corp. was born. The name was a nod to Kenmare, a small town in County Kerry, Ireland, the ancestral soil of Dan's family. But this wasn't about nostalgia. This was about money, deals, and the thrill of the hunt.

Kenmare quickly became a magnet for acquisition opportunities, with a steady flow of companies landing on our desks from investment bankers, brokers, and the occasional desperate seller. There was one issue, however: most of them were garbage. In the private equity world, the hit ratio is brutal; maybe two or three out of every hundred deals have real potential. The rest are overpriced, mismanaged, or just plain unsalvageable. But when we found something that worked, we pounced.

By the end of 1986, Kenmare had three new trophies on the shelf. First up: OMC Products, an undergarment manufacturer in Puerto Rico. Then came Old America

Stores, an arts-and-crafts retailer based in Howe, Texas, a sleepy town about 75 miles north of Dallas.

And then there was my first deal as the lead. It was a test—an opportunity to prove I could spot, negotiate, and close a deal, all without training wheels. I dove in, dissecting financials, grilling management, and cutting through the noise to find the real value. This wasn't just business—it was a game of strategy, patience, and nerve. And I was all in.

Chapter Three: Getting Into The Business

In late 1986, John Sullivan proved to be an invaluable resource when I was neck-deep into structuring the acquisition and financing documentation for the purchase of the operating assets of Abrasive Engineering and Manufacturing, Inc. (AEM) from its founder and sole shareholder. Based in Olathe, Kansas, a suburb of Kansas City, AEM specializes in manufacturing wide belt sanding and surface preparation equipment, boasting annual revenues of around $8 million. The deal itself was a $3 million transaction, financed almost entirely by a small, no-frills bank in Kansas City, Missouri. It was finalized in the closing days of December, wrapping up the year with a satisfying bow, tied neatly on it. AEM was then folded into the Pangborn North American operations, bolstering our surface preparation equipment manufacturing portfolio.

As winter thawed into spring, February and March of 1987 found me entrenched in efforts to acquire Bally Refrigeration, situated in Bally, Pennsylvania, just 15 miles from Allentown. Bally primarily churned out walk-in refrigeration systems but had recently ventured into curtain wall production for the construction sector. They banked on the idea that the same production and assembly methods would translate seamlessly. Spoiler alert: they didn't. The construction side flopped spectacularly, leaving a mess both operationally and financially.

The real dealbreaker, however, wasn't on their balance sheet. It was under their office—literally. During due diligence, we discovered a lagoon of waste materials lurking beneath the expansive manufacturing complex. Dealing with environmental remediation while trying to operate a business was, needless to say, a hard pass for us. The acquisition stalled, then died quietly, buried under layers of potential EPA headaches.

I made several trips to Bally during this time, flying into Newark, New Jersey, and enduring a two-hour drive to the plant. One Sunday evening, fresh off a flight, I slipped into the murky light of a payphone alcove near the jet bridge to make a quick call. Mid-conversation, my peripheral vision caught something. Or rather, someone – Mike Tyson.

Yes, *that* Mike Tyson.

He lumbered off the same jet bridge with a couple of teenage kids trailing behind him like mismatched bookends, seemingly part of his entourage. Tyson had just scored the World Boxing Association title against James Smith in Las Vegas the night before, March 7th, adding it to his World Boxing Council belt won from Trevor Berbick in November 1986. This was Tyson in his raw, meteoric rise—pre-champagne endorsements, pre-private jets. Just a 20-year-old phenom flying coach with championship belts slung over his broad shoulders in an X formation.

The belts were almost cartoonish in their gaudiness, made from green and purple leather (or maybe plastic), adorned with gold ornaments, some missing pins, swinging loosely as he trudged down the concourse. He wore a pair of headphones, a Sony Walkman in hand, his face still swollen and visibly still recovering from the brutal match in the ring less than 24 hours prior. It was surreal, watching this living embodiment of raw power shuffle through Newark Airport like just another weary traveler.

About five months later, Tyson would become the first undisputed heavyweight champion by defeating Tony

Tucker for the International Boxing Federation title on August 1st, 1987. He turned 21 just weeks before, on June 30th. But on that night in Newark, he was just Mike, a force of nature hiding in plain sight, battered but unbroken, walking beside me like it was the most ordinary thing in the world.

As the first quarter of 1987 came to a close, my collaboration with Gil Raker was a watershed moment in my professional life. Working outside the confines of our office was refreshing, but what made it truly memorable was Gil himself. He was in his early forties, with olive-toned skin, jet-black hair that seemed immune to graying, and piercing blue eyes that could dissect a financial statement with a single glimpse. Gil was the epitome of a financial savant – acute, meticulous, and always three steps ahead in any negotiation.

Gil lived in Greenwich, Connecticut, and had a BA in Chemistry and Mathematics from Eastern College, an MBA in Production Management, and a PhD in Finance from Syracuse University. He was the kind of guy whose resume made you sit up a little straighter. Nonetheless, despite his success, I sensed a sort of restlessness in him, like he was biding his time for the next big thing. It wasn't a matter of *if* he'd move on, but *when*.

Our target was Unit Rig, a subsidiary of Kendavis Industries International, Inc., part of the chaotic empire led by T. Cullen Davis and his brothers, who received equal shares of their father's estate upon his death in 1968. Davis wasn't just an oil heir from Fort Worth, Texas; he was tabloid fodder, notorious for his acquittals on murder charges and allegations of attempting to hire a hitman in the 1970s. He was first accused of murdering the daughter of his estranged wife, Priscilla, and her boyfriend. Davis was believed to be the wealthiest man ever tried for murder in the U.S.

The prosecution claimed that Davis forced Priscilla's 12-year-old daughter, Andrea, into the basement of their mansion, made her kneel, and then shot her dead. They also alleged that he went on to shoot Priscilla's live-in boyfriend, Stan Farr, a former basketball star at Texas Christian University. Despite these accusations, a Texas jury found Davis not guilty of the murders. Davis and Pricilla were in the process of divorcing during the time when the murders occurred. Following the trial, the prosecutor said, "We were out-bought and out-thought."

Two years later, he was acquitted of attempting to hire a hit man to kill both Pricilla and the judge overseeing his divorce. Clearly, Davis's reputation as a devoted family man and successful businessman was questionable at best.

However, it was later reported that Davis became a Christian associated with televangelist James Robison.

Unit Rig, based in Tulsa, Oklahoma, manufactured colossal off-highway dump trucks under the Lectra Haul brand. These weren't your average trucks; they were behemoths powered by four gigantic General Electric wheel motors and a diesel generator. The company was drowning in inventory, with $70 million worth of wheel motors alone gathering dust. I remember the painstaking process of copying inventory data onto my Compaq computer, which devoured about a dozen floppy disks of mine. It was a digital slog that felt almost medieval by today's standards.

Adding to the mix, Oral Roberts was across town, perched in his Prayer Tower, famously declaring that God would "call him home" if he didn't raise $8 million for his ministry. While the televangelist secured millions through faith and fear, we scrambled to piece together a financial offer that wouldn't make seasoned investors laugh us out of the room.

Regardless of our efforts, Unit Rig slipped through our fingers. We were outgunned by industry giants like Manitowoc, whose deep pockets and strategic advantages made our meticulously constructed "bootstrap" offer look like spare change. Gil, however, didn't lose a wink of sleep over it. Shortly after, he moved on to become a Managing

Director at Ditri Associates, Inc., chasing the bigger and better opportunities we all knew were waiting for him.

On a particularly hot day in June 1987, I remember sitting at the poolside at The Breakers in Palm Beach, Florida, enjoying the sun with my girlfriend, soon-to-be fiancée, Lynn, a stunning, down-to-earth woman who grew up on a farm in Paris, Illinois. Life, at that point, was smooth sailing, the kind of easiness that comes with warm weather, cool drinks, and zero obligations. That is, until Dan reached out to me. He had an urgent assignment, one he wanted me to lead. His first question was, *"Do you have a passport?"* I knew what was coming next, but I didn't mind.

Then, came, *"Would you mind cutting your Florida trip short?"*

I didn't mind that either.

Dan told me to coordinate with his brother John for a meeting at the Rockefeller Plaza passport office the next day. Just like that, my vacation was cut short. We then packed up, flew back to St. Louis, and I threw together a bag for what I thought would be a routine, week-long work trip. Little did I know, I was about to jump headfirst into something much more convoluted.

Landing in New York, I met up with John. Fortunately, he had a family friend interning at Kenmare who'd been standing in line at the passport office for me. That meant that I didn't have to wait the usual 2–3 hours that it takes. Passport secured, I caught a cab to the office, where Dan and John laid it all out: Pangborn's senior managers in Europe had made a serious $10 million offer to buy out the European operations, and I was the guy they wanted to seal the deal.

$10 million was a hefty number, especially considering that Europe's revenue and profits didn't hold a candle to our North American operations. But this wasn't just about the sale, it was a chance to pay down some debt and fatten up Kenmare's bank account. *No pressure, right?*

Within 48 hours of that poolside call in Florida, I was on a helicopter from the 34th Street heliport to JFK with John by my side. A TWA 747 carried us across the Atlantic, landing us in London around 8:00 AM local time. Business class or not, sleep had been elusive. Jetlag hit me like a freight train, the first time I'd ever experienced it, full-force.

We breezed through customs, grabbed a cab, and headed straight to Clifford Chance, our solicitors (because in the UK, "lawyers" apparently wasn't posh enough). John introduced me to all the key players. I nodded, smiled, took notes, the whole nine yards. But mentally, I was running on fumes. Then came the tea. I'd never really been a tea drinker, but after several cups, I realized British tea packs a serious caffeine punch. I was practically vibrating.

After a long day of meetings, we checked into the Sheraton Belgravia. Over dinner, John hit me with a curveball: an urgent, entirely unavoidable meeting in Italy. He slid a plane ticket across the table and told me: *"We'll take a cab to Heathrow together. You're flying to Milan. I'm heading back to New York. You've got this now. You'll be fine. Just don't let them push you around."*

Three days ago, I was lounging in Florida. Now, I'd been catapulted into international deal-making, navigating London's left-side driving, and gearing up to hop over to Italy, solo. And, it struck me: I wasn't going home anytime soon. And this wasn't just another business trip.

As I boarded the plane, I took a deep breath. Italy. Another first. I had barely wrapped my head around being in London, and now I was heading to one of the world's most glamorous countries, not for sightseeing, but to lock down a multi-million-dollar transaction. The stakes were sky-high.

The flight was a blur, and 2 hours later, I was in Milan. All the passengers disembarked directly onto the tarmac, and as we made our way toward the terminal, the security was impossible to miss. Armed police with machine guns were stationed everywhere. As I approached the gate, an administrative employee of the company was waiting for me in a slick suit and sunglasses, in European businessman fashion. He barely spoke English, but he didn't need to. He took my bag, and motioned for me to follow, and within minutes we jumped into his Fiat, cutting through Milan's chaotic streets and traffic seamlessly as we began our drive about 30 minutes north to the plant in Caronno Pertusella. It felt good to be back on the right side of the road, and the scenery was stunning.

After meeting the General Manager, we exchanged some small talk about my background and recent travels. When I asked if he had the latest monthly financial statement available for me to review, he grinned and said, "Ah, now I know why you're here! They're going to sell the company!" The memory of the last sale process under Standard Oil was clearly still fresh for him. And he was spot on; the plan indeed was to sell.

By the time I left the building that evening, my head was spinning, but I felt good. I had held my own. The Italians knew they weren't dealing with a rookie. I grabbed a drink at the hotel bar, took a deep breath, and let it sink in.

And so, I spent the next few days diving into the financials and operations, getting a solid grasp of the business. The employees were incredible; warm, welcoming, and eager to show me around. Every evening after work, we'd head out for drinks and dinner at hidden local gems far from the usual tourist spots. We even ventured further north to breathtaking places like Lake Como and across the border into Switzerland. It was an unforgettable experience, both professionally and personally.

Soon after returning to London, I checked back into the Sheraton Belgravia. London felt oddly familiar, but I wasn't complaining. The doorman gave me a nod like we were old friends, and the bartender remembered my drink. The hotel bar and restaurant were a lifesaver all weekend, especially on Friday night when I was completely wiped out. After a quick meal and a drink, I crashed. I slept in late both Saturday and Sunday, finally feeling well-rested. Each afternoon, I set out to explore the city, taking in the sights, enjoying the lively streets, and soaking up as much of London as I could.

On Monday morning, I caught a train for a three-hour ride north to Ossett, West Yorkshire, to visit the Pangborn operation known as Spencer and Halstead, Ltd. The plant was tucked away in the middle of farm country, and the office they set me up in had a window overlooking a field of sheep, a remarkable change from the busy streets of London.

The management team here was a different breed compared to the animated crew in Italy. They were the ones working on the acquisition deal with a public company called W.A. Tyzack, Plc., and let's just say they weren't exactly the 'drinks after work' type. Leading the charge was Gary Bennett, a huge guy with an ego to match. He was strictly business, and no fluff.

There were no wild nights out or hidden gems to explore after hours, but the team was polite enough, which was all I really needed. I spent a few days digging into the business and getting a handle on the finances. Once I had what I needed, I hopped back on the train to London and checked into the Sheraton Belgravia again, ready for the next round.

In the middle of all this corporate chaos, life back home kept moving forward. In August, I flew back to St. Louis for a brief but unforgettable intermission: my wedding to Lynn. We'd bought a charming, center-hall colonial a few months before I was thrown into the whirlwind of the Pangborn assignment. It had the kind of white picket fence you'd expect from a storybook. We had it installed right after moving in. That little fence framed a backyard gathering of about 25 close family and friends. It wasn't a grand affair in the least. There were no extravagant venues or wedding planners. No, it was just heartfelt vows exchanged under an open sky, with laughter spilling out of red Solo cups and the kind of warmth that doesn't need fancy decorations.

The morning after the wedding, however, I was back in business mode, boarding a direct flight later that afternoon from St. Louis to London Gatwick. But the exhaustion hit me hard. I remember the stewardess offering me a glass of champagne as soon as I settled into my seat. I took a polite sip, leaned back, and the next thing I knew, the plane's wheels were locking into position for landing. I was out like a light, and if I'm being honest, that was probably the best sleep I'd gotten in months.

A week later, Lynn joined me in London for what we optimists called our "working honeymoon." Not exactly sunsets on the Amalfi Coast, but we made the best of it, squeezing in quality time between boardrooms and business dinners. We'd have late-night strolls along the Thames, grabbing fish and chips wrapped in newspaper, pretending for an hour or two that we were just another couple on vacation, not tethered to spreadsheets the whole time.

After Lynn returned to the States, it was back to the grind. Aside from a brief stint in New York in October, I was mostly on my own, shuttling between London and Italy, preparing due diligence information and responses to questions from the buyer, deal structuring, and the endless back-and-forth that comes with high-stakes transactions. I even scouted other acquisition opportunities in England and Germany, chasing leads that fizzled out before they could catch fire.

Finally, in mid-December 1987, the Pangborn deal closed. No confetti cannons or champagne showers; just a stack of signed documents, firm handshakes, and a sense of accomplishment that settled over me like a well-worn coat. The numbers lined up, the stakeholders were satisfied, and we'd managed to turn a multifaceted, multi-country operation into a smooth and calculated success. Sometimes, the best stories aren't the ones you plan. They're the ones you live through, one unexpected detour at a time.

Chapter Four: Going into Hyperdrive

At the beginning of 1988, John Sullivan left Kenmare to carve his own path, seemingly tired of living in the shadow of his older brother's spotlight. When he left, the change was seismic. I got paired with Bill Laverty, a man nearly 40 years my senior who had worked alongside Dan for over two decades. Bill was a Boston Irish Catholic with experience in engineering and physics. His passion on the side, however, was the racetrack, the streets, and a lifetime of experience. You would always find him at the Off-Track Betting parlor, betting away as if his life depended on it. He chain-smoked Pall Malls, drank hard liquor, and swore like a sailor. All that said, he was one of the most astute minds I'd ever met.

Bill taught me a boatload of things that I don't think I could ever forget, even if I tried. He believed in keeping things simple: *Never get involved with a business you don't understand.* That lesson alone was worth gold. While I had a strong grip on the financial side of deals, Bill had me climbing a steep learning curve on operations. He pushed me to look past the numbers and connect the balance sheets and income statements to the actual pulse of the business. Two years in, the tables turned. I had him on his own crash course in finance and accounting, teaching him how to project financial outcomes based on operational realities. It started as a mentor-mentee relationship, but soon enough, we were pushing each other to be sharper, better, and always one step ahead.

Bill lived in Osterville on Cape Cod with Margaret, his wife of nearly 50 years. She was the picture of elegance; always in a dress, with opalescent pearls adorning her décolletage. Every week, Bill voyaged to New York all the way from the Hyannis airport, and I would fly in from St. Louis. Kenmare put us up in a two-bedroom apartment on 29th and 3rd Avenue, just a few blocks from the office. Most weeks, we arrived Monday morning and left Friday afternoon. Some weeks, we never left at all. New York was an experience in itself. Bill often sat next to actress Lee Remick on his Cape-bound flights, while I often found myself next to Joe Corr, the president of TWA. But the real action started when we landed.

Nearly every single night, we wined and dined at Piccolo Mondo, a classic spot on 69th and 1st Avenue. Bill had been a regular for years, and soon, I was too. We knew everyone there—Aldo, the towering German bartender in his seventies, always ready with my *second first drink* before we even finished the first. Carlo, the manager, never handed us a menu. Whatever we wanted, the chef very graciously whipped up for us. Carlo was a spectacle all on his own. A slightly heavyset, charming Italian bachelor in his forties, he reveled in sharing tales of his latest escapades, particularly his rendezvous with the lonely wives of Manhattan executives, whom he entertained in the so-called *basement* downstairs.

Piccolo Mondo was filled with its own unforgettable characters. Out of all of them, Vladimir Horowitz, the Maestro himself, arguably takes the cake. The legendary Russian-born pianist always arrived with his family, who would take their places at the far end of the dining room, waiting for him to make his grand entrance—alone, dramatic, and timed to perfection. Then there was Mr. Jack, a five-foot-tall bookie with an unmistakable Brooklyn accent that was so thick you could spread it on toast. He had been running bets in the city longer than we'd been alive. Sometimes we invited him to our table, bought his dinner, and listened to him ramble about the odds. One night, we decided to take him out for his 75th birthday, hiring a limo to the Meadowlands racetrack in New Jersey. As we entered the Lincoln Tunnel, he started panicking.

"I ain't left Manhattan in fifty years!"

The man was practically hyperventilating. The city was his entire world. And for a night, we got to watch him step beyond it.

This was just how life was with Bill: an education in business, people, and the art of navigating both. The deals were important, but the lessons, the people, and the stories? That was the real gold.

In the same year, 1988, Bill and I eventually found ourselves working separately on two major acquisitions in the commercial refrigeration industry. Bill locked in a $17 million deal for the walk-in cooler business from The Vollrath Company in River Falls, Wisconsin, while I negotiated a $27 million acquisition of the Kolpak walk-in cooler and McCall reach-in cooler businesses from Jack Dalton in Parsons, Tennessee.

Jack Dalton was, by far, one of the most dynamic businessmen whose path I had ever crossed. He was, however, so much more than that. He and Dan had crossed paths years earlier when Dan controlled some of the biggest players in the food-service equipment industry. Jack, always one to think big, had built an impressive refrigeration empire, but his management style was more *go big or go broke* than sound financial planning. Growth was his obsession, and he funded it with an ever-growing pile of debt. The numbers didn't lie—he needed help. And in Dan, he saw a man with the resources (and nerve) to turn things around.

Jack didn't do anything small. He lived in the heart of Parsons in what was, without question, the biggest house for ten counties. Every day, he rolled up to his plant in a massive dark green Rolls-Royce, parking it right at the main entrance—just in case anyone forgot who was in charge. He was more than just a local big shot; he had serious political ties and sat on the University of Tennessee's board of trustees.

During due diligence, our team put together a strategy to tighten up operations and bring the business back to profitability. The goal was simple: refine the company, stabilize cash flow, and make the acquisition appealing enough for a traditional commercial bank to finance it. But there was a catch; Dan still needed to come up with the equity component to satisfy the bank's terms.

That's where things got interesting.

You see, Dan had this unique gift. He could be bold, relentless, and, at times, wildly persuasive, all while getting people to make decisions that defied all reason and logic. This time, his target was Jack's minority equity partner, Hisham Araim. Somehow, Dan convinced Hisham to roll over his share of the net proceeds from the sale—plus a little extra—into the newly formed entity Kenmare was using to acquire the business.

But here was the kicker: Hisham's contribution covered the *entire* equity amount the bank required, yet he only walked away with a 20% stake in the new commercial refrigeration group. Mathematically, it made no sense at all. But Dan had this way of making even the most lopsided deals sound like the opportunity of a lifetime. It was the kind of move that made you shake your head—and maybe take notes. Dan had pulled off another deal, one that defied all expectations, and just like that, Kenmare had a brand-new refrigeration empire under its belt.

It was a masterstroke, the kind of deal that left everyone wondering how Dan managed to pull it off—except by now, we'd stopped wondering. He had a knack for bending situations to his will, turning long shots into sure things. And with that, the refrigeration empire was his. And so, with the ink barely dry on the deal, it was time to get more acquainted with the new territory. That meant regular trips to Parsons, Tennessee, a place about as far culturally from Wall Street as you could get.

Parsons wasn't exactly a luxury destination. Smack in the middle of nowhere, about ten miles south of Highway 40, it sat equidistant from Memphis and Nashville and was at least two hours in either direction. And in case anyone needed a drink after the long drive, which we often did, well, tough luck. Parsons was in a dry county.

Luckily, the company had a workaround, a spacious, four-bedroom cabin nestled on the edge of a lake. It was rustic but comfortable, with a massive stone fireplace in the great room and a screened-in porch that offered a peaceful view of the water. And one of the best parts: the kitchen was fully stocked, and not just with food. Hidden behind the pantry was a deep closet, crammed with every kind of liquor known to mankind—1.75-liter bottles of all the good stuff lined the shelves like trophies. Then there was the McCall refrigeration equipment, fully loaded with beer and anything else that might take the edge off a long day.

Food runs meant a trip to the local Piggly Wiggly, the small-town grocery chain where the aisles smelled like fried chicken with a hint of bargain-brand laundry detergent. One of our lawyers, a sharp guy from the East Coast who happened to be Jewish, wasn't entirely convinced he was even *allowed* through the front door. His wife packed kosher food for him before he made his *one and only* trip to Parsons, and after that, he politely declined all future visits.

When visiting Kolpak, I usually flew into Nashville instead of Memphis; there were simply more convenient flight options. On one such trip, I found myself seated at the front of the plane, across the aisle from none other than country music legend Randy Travis and a woman I assumed was his manager. We exchanged a few brief words—both were gracious, polite, and low-key.

The humorous part of the encounter came after we landed. Randy, his manager, and I were the first to deplane. As we walked through the concourse, they were a few strides ahead of me when another passenger caught up and asked, "Hey, was that Al Unser, Jr.?"

I nearly lost it. For context, Al Unser Jr.—or "Little Al"—was a celebrated IndyCar driver and the son of the legendary Al Unser Sr., a four-time Indy 500 winner. Al Jr. had won two Indy 500s himself. I suppose there was a passing resemblance between the two, but as a longtime IndyCar fan, I had to hold back a laugh before politely replying, "No... that was Randy Travis."

On another trip—this time heading from St. Louis to Parsons, Tennessee via Nashville—I boarded the plane and found myself sitting next to Johnny Rodriguez, a major name in country music, and what seemed to be a member of his band. At the time, I had no idea who he was. We exchanged some light conversation across the aisle before the captain came over the intercom to announce a mechanical issue. Everyone had to deplane.

Johnny turned to me and said, "Come grab a drink with us." We headed to the bar nearest the gate and ended up having a couple of great hours together while we waited for the delayed flight. They were both warm, funny, and generous—Johnny even picked up the tab. It wasn't until later that I learned he was one of the most successful Hispanic artists in country music, with a string of hits to his name.

I think not knowing who he was might have been refreshing for him. It wasn't fan worship, just three guys sitting at an airport bar, killing time and having fun. Sometimes, those are the best kinds of encounters.

While things settled in Tennessee, I was busy wrapping up two new acquisitions. First up was Jackson Products, a Tampa-based commercial dishwashing machine manufacturer, snagged from Alco Standard for $10 million. Almost immediately after, I finalized the Welbilt Refrigeration deal—a $5 million acquisition that added a new walk-in refrigeration plant in the City of Industry, just outside Los Angeles.

The Jackson acquisition, however, was a game of cold, hard tactics. The real plan, which was kept behind closed doors, was to flip it. Dan had an old friend who needed a new project, and that friend just happened to be Jack Dalton. Within a year, Jackson Products changed hands again, this time to Jack, at a modest profit. A tidy little deal, just as planned.

The Welbilt acquisition, on the other hand, was a long-term move, and a damn good one at that. Before this deal, our refrigeration business had a serious logistical problem: shipping bulky, walk-in coolers over the mountains was a nightmare. Now, with manufacturing plants in Wisconsin, Tennessee, and California, we have regional coverage, cutting costs and delivery times.

Standardization was next. We standardized tooling and hardware across all three plants, bringing them under one brand: Kolpak. The McCall reach-in coolers were stocked in each facility for fast shipping, and just like that, The Shannon Group was born in 1989 – a streamlined, practically coast-to-coast refrigeration powerhouse. Three years, four acquisitions, and a brand-new empire – suffice to say that things were smooth sailing from there; at least I had thought as much, but then came Detroit Tool.

The Detroit Tool deal was a headache from the very beginning. The sellers, whose family problems were enough to send them into a spiral, couldn't agree on a single thing. Half of them wanted out, the other half wanted to bleed the business for every dollar it was worth, and their attorneys were as crooked as a dog's hind leg. The St. Louis-based legal team representing them pushed every ethical boundary they could find, playing games, stalling negotiations, and trying to squeeze more money out of us at every turn. It was brutal, ugly, and exhausting. But I didn't back down.

Through a relentless series of all-night negotiating sessions, exchanges that tested every ounce of patience I had left, and a few well-placed tactical moves, I finally locked in the Letter of Intent. But that was only half the battle. The real challenge was getting them to the closing table and securing the financing for a $36 million transaction, including $6 million from the sellers themselves.

Then came a tip from an employee. A totally unexpected curveball. Outside, beneath the soil in a field behind one of the buildings that sprawled across the town of Lebanon, were silos (trenches) full of industrial waste generated over decades of production operations. An environmental wasteland on a 28-acre property containing metal shavings, cutting fluids, and paint sludge, all without so much as a mention of it by the principals, their investment bankers, or their legal team.

After weeks of discussions, negotiations, battling back and forth on deal terms, including some ridiculous counters from the other side, I knew we needed to, eventually, come to terms on how to settle a resolution to this issue as well. I had my eye on the prize. Get control of this beast and make it roar! So, I had to be delicate dealing with the other side on this timely and thankful whisper to not crater the deal.

It was a balance between calling the other side out for the deception and a need to remain friendly on my way to the finish line. I approached the other side very calmly, stating that we needed an environmental assessment of the properties after learning about past waste disposal processes. The other side acted surprised and reluctantly agreed to have Woodward-Clyde Consultants perform a Phase I analysis of the property.

The investigation confirmed the existence of the materials and a clean-up estimate ranging from $800 thousand to $1.2 million. The provisions of the Purchase Agreement we were negotiating relating to the indemnifications made by the Sellers in favor of the Purchaser were amended, and the amount of the escrowed funds in respect of the Seller's representations and warranties was adjusted upward to $3.8 million. My trade-off, in return for the substantial increase in the escrowed funds and to finally get the deal done, was a cost-sharing arrangement by the parties for claims against the escrow as follows:

	Sellers	Purchaser
First $2.0 Million	100%	0%
Next $1.5 Million	75%	25%
Next $0.3 Million	50%	50%
Above $3.8 Million	0%	100%

The deal finally closed on July 28, 1989, on Bill's 70th birthday. I remember looking across the table at him, wondering if this was really how he wanted to spend his big day. He didn't seem to mind. A closed deal was the only kind of present he needed.

From the outside, Detroit Tool and Engineering looked like a powerhouse. It manufactured highly specialized production equipment; machines that global giants like General Electric, Goodyear Tire, and Procter & Gamble depended on. But under the hood, it was a mess. The family had been running it like a piggy bank, sucking out profits while refusing to reinvest in the business. They were sitting on a goldmine and didn't even know it. But we did.

During the due diligence period, we mapped out a plan that the sellers had been too short-sighted to execute themselves. The right capital expenditures could double revenue overnight in the most profitable segment of the business. And better yet, we didn't even have to foot the bill. We structured deals with our biggest customers so they would finance our expansion for us. Deposits and progress payments were built directly into the contracts. That meant new equipment, plant expansions, and working capital—all without using our own money.

Six months after closing, Detroit Tool Group, Inc. had raked in over $15 million in cash. That was after we covered the costs of expansion. The business was printing money, all because we knew how to unlock its potential.

Every acquisition Bill and I made followed a set pattern. We weren't looking for high-risk, high-tech ventures or trendy startups that could vanish overnight. We went after businesses with a specific profile—high know-how, low-tech manufacturing. They were stable, they had strong competitive positions, and they made things people actually needed.

The formula was simple. Step one: Install a new CEO and CFO. No exceptions. The old leadership had to go. Step two: demand clean, accurate financials—fast. No guessing, no waiting. Step three: stay hands-on. We weren't the kind of owners who hid behind spreadsheets. We walked the floors, we asked questions, and we made sure things ran the way they were supposed to.

Detroit Tool had been a fight from start to finish, but it was worth it. Another piece of the empire was locked in. And there were plenty more moves to make.

Chapter Five: Arrival at the Peak

While Bill and I were deep in the trenches, building and managing our manufacturing empire, the rest of the team at Kenmare wasn't just standing around collecting dust. They were making moves, big ones, as they branched out into industries that had nothing to do with manufacturing. Up until a couple of years earlier, Dan had been laser-focused on traditional businesses, with only a handful of exceptions, such as CPC Industries and Old America Stores. But now, Kenmare was rewriting its own playbook.

Robert Silva had stepped into Gil Raker's role as Executive VP after his departure in '87, working closely with Dan and Andrew Mayer—Dan's longtime right-hand man and controller from his old investment firm. Bob was no rookie. He'd done his time in private equity and had cut his teeth in commercial lending at a big New York bank before joining Kenmare. Together, this trio was making waves, taking on acquisitions that pushed Kenmare into uncharted waters—retail chains, post-production services, anything that looked like an opportunity. Yellow Front Stores, Bonanza, Family Bargain Centers, Compact Video Services, Manhattan Transfer & Edit—none of it was familiar territory, but that didn't stop them.

By mid-1989, Kenmare's empire had swelled to a staggering $700 million in combined revenues. The manufacturing arm—Detroit Tool, The Shannon Group, Jackson Products, Pangborn, and AEM—accounted for about $250 million. Retail, including Yellow Front, Bonanza, Old America, and Family Bargain Centers, made up a hefty $400 million. Post-production, the wildcard of the portfolio, contributed another $50 million. Kenmare had transformed from a manufacturing powerhouse into a diversified machine, and we were all along for the ride.

And the incentives? Let's just say Dan knew how to keep his team happy. Everyone at Kenmare had a stake, a phantom stock ownership plan that gave us real skin in the game. If we acquired and managed a company, we got 4% of it. If we weren't directly involved, we still got a cut of 1%. It was a setup that ensured we weren't just working for a paycheck; we were building our own fortunes. Add in the sky-high salaries, uncapped expense accounts, and fat success bonuses tied to acquisitions and exits, and you have a team of hungry, motivated dealmakers ready to go to war for the next big win.

Of course, the price of playing the game at this level wasn't just measured in dollar signs. Work wasn't work anymore; it was life. I was on the road 50 weeks a year, bouncing between New York, St. Louis, and whatever city held the next opportunity. I was in boardrooms, on factory floors, inside retail stores, cutting deals over steak dinners and whiskey. It was thrilling, invigorating, and relentless. A normal family life? That was for the ordinary person, which certainly wasn't me. You didn't just do this job; you *became* it.

And then there was Dan. From the outside, his St. Louis life seemed picture-perfect. But the more time I spent in this world, the more I saw through the cracks. Besides acquiring companies, Kenmare wasn't just creating a reality of its own, one where ambition ruled and personal lives took a back seat. I was thriving, but at what cost? And was Dan's life really what he wanted me to aspire to?

Come November 1989. We were in the final stretch of closing the sale of Pangborn North America to a division of Merrill Lynch. It was a $30 million deal, and after paying off debt and other closing costs, Kenmare stood to walk away with a cool $5 million. Not bad for an asset we'd acquired four years earlier, where we had already squeezed out profits at every turn—$1 million at the initial closing, another $6 million from selling the European operations (after paying down $4 million in debt), and an extra $3 million in management fees along the way. By all accounts, this was already a win.

Then, Dan pulled one of his classic last-minute moves. His golden rule: *You don't get what you don't ask for.* And this time, he was about to prove it again.

Buried in the $25 million of debt and closing expenses was $1 million in capitalized equipment leases—long-term obligations that typically fell on the seller at closing. It was standard practice. I had already hammered out the final structure of the deal, and Merrill Lynch was ready to wrap it up. Then, just before we signed, Dan threw out a simple but sharp adjustment: "Get them to take on the leases."

His logic was bulletproof. To Merrill Lynch, it was a minor tweak—bumping their purchase price from $30 million to $31 million, a modest 3.3% increase. Barely a ripple in their world. But for us? That extra million meant our net take-home from the sale jumped from $5 million to $6 million, which was a massive 20% boost to our final payout. It took one phone call, which lasted less than a minute of negotiation. Merrill barely blinked before agreeing, and just like that, we walked away with an extra million dollars at closing.

It was the kind of move that defined Dan, and one that stuck with me. Most people accept the terms they're given, happy to close a solid deal. But the real players push the boundaries, ask for more, and find ways to create extra value where others don't even think to look. That's how Kenmare operated, and that's why we kept winning. The lesson I learned in the end: never leave money on the table, and never assume the deal is final until you've tested every angle. Because if you don't ask, you definitely won't get.

Before we sealed the deal with Merrill Lynch, we had one last round of tire-kickers sniffing around Pangborn North America. Gary Bennett and his colleague from W.A. Tyzack Plc—the same company that had scooped up Spencer and Halstead, Ltd. and the Pangborn operation in Italy in 87—wanted a closer look. They were considering a bid, so we set up a tour. First stop: Mississauga, just outside Toronto.

I met them at the Ritz, and from the jump, something felt out of sorts. A couple of years earlier, when we were in England, I was the guy from the holding company, and naturally, I picked up the dinner tabs, rental cars, and maybe even the hotel. Again, standard practice. But this time, Gary had been cut loose from Kenmare for nearly two years. He was supposed to be a big shot now, but somehow, I was still footing the bill.

The dinner and hotel were both on me. *Alright, fine. No biggie,* I thought, at the time. Then came round two in Washington, D.C., where we checked into the Watergate before heading to Pangborn's Hagerstown plant. Rental car? Dinner? Hotel? Again – courtesy of *me*. At this point, it wasn't just odd; it was becoming a pattern, one that began to irk me. So, my suspicions grew.

The final leg of the trip was New York City to meet with Dan. At least there, I had an escape route – my own apartment – so they had to cover their own rooms. But before I was off the hook, there was one last stop: Peter Luger Steakhouse in Brooklyn. And this? This was going to be a scene. So, we went all in.

First, cocktails. Then, the famous Luger sliced tomatoes and onions drenched in their signature sauce. Jumbo shrimp cocktail – extra-large, of course. Then, came the main event: USDA prime beef, cooked to absolute perfection. Dessert, more drinks – the full show.

By the time the dust settled, three hours had passed, and the check was, well... let's just say it looked more like a phone number than a dinner bill. And just like clockwork, Gary motioned for the server to pass it to me. I reached for my credit card, ready to take one last hit.

Then the waiter hit me with it: *"Sorry, sir, we only accept Peter Luger credit cards or cash."*

I had maybe fifty bucks on me. No Peter Luger card. No way out. For the first time on the whole trip, Gary had to open his own wallet, for a change. And when he pulled out that thick stack of cash, I could practically feel his soul leaving his body. It *had* to be killing him.

I sat back, utterly amused, watching the moment unfold. That was the real test. If they wouldn't even *invest* in their own damn meals, there was no way they were coughing up the money we wanted for Pangborn. And sure enough, after our meeting with Dan the next morning, they disappeared into thin air. It taught me one thing, though: if someone won't pick up a check, they sure as hell won't pick up a company.

By the time 1989 was winding down, I wasn't just keeping up, I was thriving. Every deal, every late-night number crunch, every negotiation had sharpened me into a real player in this game. It was a long way from where I started in 1985, staring at my first big opportunity: Shasta Beverages. Back then, it was owned by Consolidated Foods, and they were eager to sell. Part of their pitch was a little fruit drink in a pouch with a straw called Capri Sun. They had high hopes for it, betting big on its U.S. rollout. But to me, it looked like a gimmick. Something about poking a hole in a foil pouch just didn't scream *big business.* We passed. Not that it really mattered—Shasta was probably too big for us at the time, and it wasn't in our wheelhouse anyway.

Turns out that Capri Sun, named after the Isle of Capri, was already a monster hit in Europe. I had no clue then, but it would go on to become one of the most famous drink brands in the world. I suppose sometimes, the biggest opportunities are the ones you don't see coming.

But I wasn't dwelling on missed chances. My real value was in the numbers—running the deep-dive analysis that made or broke deals. I built and refined a *Lotus 1-2-3* financial model that became our go-to for evaluating acquisitions, which was also used by the analysts Kenmare later hired as the portfolio expanded in support of Dan, Bob, and Andy. It wasn't just a spreadsheet; it was a crystal ball.

The model covered everything. It tracked every dollar, from where it was coming from to where it was going. Sources and uses of cash were the foundation of every deal. Income statements laid out the past, present, and projected future in a way that told a clear story. Profit on paper meant nothing if cash flow wasn't there to back it up, so projections had to be airtight. Balance sheets offered a full financial snapshot, while debt repayment schedules ensured every lender got what they were owed, down to the last cent.

Collateral calculations were a game of leverage, literally. Banks didn't just want to know what they could lend; they wanted to know what they could take back if things went south. Cost of goods sold and Selling, General and Administrative expenses. Expenses stripped the business down to its raw costs, exposing inefficiencies and hidden opportunities. But the real bottom line was the internal rate of return. At the end of the day, it wasn't about revenue or even profit. It was about how much money we were actually making and how hard every dollar was working.

As Kenmare grew, so did our operation. We expanded into the other half of the 20th floor at 1 Madison Avenue, bringing in new analysts to keep up with the deal flow. My model became so effective that one of our main investment bankers, Rodman & Renshaw in Chicago, asked if they could use it for their clients. I took that as a compliment.

But it wasn't just numbers. I spent hours in the thick of it with lawyers, dissecting contracts, structuring deals, and figuring out every loophole, every angle. But there was something I didn't know back then. The very skills I was honing—the art of negotiation, the ability to see the weak spots in a deal—would one day become my weapons in a much bigger battle, one against the very people who had taught me the game.

Meanwhile, Dan and I were getting tight, at least, professionally. One meeting with him wasn't just a quick sit-down in his office; it was an ongoing, never-ending, and all-consuming mission. We started at his desk, moved to the black service car, straight through the airport terminal, past the ticket counter, down the concourse, and onto the shuttle to Boston. He kept going; I turned around and caught the next flight back to New York. That was just how things worked with Dan. If he had something to discuss, you were going to hear it—wherever, whenever.

He was brilliant and ruthless with numbers. I could spend hours refining a fifty-page financial model, and in under a minute, he'd find the one mistake I missed. It was uncanny, almost unnatural. He had a mind built for the game, and he played it hard. His travel schedule was relentless, and so were his expenses. He charged everything from flights, hotels, dinners, and all the way to company events on his personal AmEx card. Every December, he covered the entire Christmas party at Piccolo Mondo, complete with a stay at the Waldorf Astoria for the key people running the portfolio companies and their spouses.

His American Express bills didn't come in envelopes; they arrived in boxes. Fifty grand a month, sometimes more.

That gold card of his had been through so many old-school credit card imprint machines that it looked warped and burnt, like a potato chip left too close to the fire. But it never got declined. Neither did Dan.

Chapter Six: The Slide

Something about Dan was changing. At first, it was subtle, trivial things that were easy to miss if you weren't looking closely enough. But once you noticed, you couldn't unsee it. But by the end of 1989, they were impossible to ignore.

For one, Dan's wife, Karen, was nowhere to be seen at that year's Christmas party. Instead, he showed up with his new girlfriend, Ann. No explanation or fanfare. Just a quiet swap. It wasn't the only surprise. Dan, always a creature of habit, never deviated from his signature meal: pounded, pan-fried Steak Diane. It didn't matter where we were, what kind of restaurant it was, or what the chef recommended. If they didn't have it, he found a way to make them cook it.

Then, there was the real estate. A condo in San Francisco that he had bought for another woman, someone he described as a "close acquaintance." And then there was the red phone—a dedicated line, installed right in his office, sitting in plain sight for everyone to see. Whenever it rang, he'd answer without a second's hesitation. And the moment he spoke, his voice morphed into something softer, something different—something none of us had ever heard before.

Then came the ad.

Lynn, the administrative assistant we shared, let it slip to me after one of Dan's breakups. He'd placed an ad in *The Village Voice*, something along the lines of, *"Wealthy financier seeks..."* He waited for responses, but to his dismay, none came; not even one. Weeks passed, which turned into months. Ghost town. He upped his therapy sessions, convinced that something was wrong. How could this be?

As it turns out, there was another Daniel J. Sullivan in the building at 1 Madison Avenue! And all the responses—bags of them—were going to him. When the mix-up was finally revealed, the doorman wheeled in sack after sack of mail, dumping them at Dan's office like a scene straight out of *Miracle on 34th Street*. It should have been funny, and maybe it was. But to Dan, it was just another reminder that things weren't quite going his way.

That fall, I flew to the West Coast to visit Welbilt. It was a rare trip where I wasn't expected to show up in a suit, and I was looking forward to it. The Brody family, who had built the business from the ground up before selling it to Kenmare, operated in a laid-back environment. That meant no ties and no dress codes – just business.

One afternoon, Dan called. He needed me at dinner in Beverly Hills with the top two guys from Compact Video Group. He was worried things weren't going well and wanted my read on the situation. I agreed, but it came at a cost: I had to bail on a Dodgers game with the Brody family, something I had been looking forward to a great deal. And, because Kenmare's unwritten rule was that important dinners required formal attire, I found myself racing to a department store to buy a shirt, tie, and sports coat on my way to dinner.

Compact Video had been acquired from Technicolor, which was owned by Ron Perelman's Andrews Group. I had heard plenty of stories about their legendary deal-making—like how one of Perelman's right-hand guys once got a pedicure *during* a high-stakes negotiation, completely rattling the other side. Or how a courier carrying a $30 million cashier's check got stuck in traffic for hours, delaying a $60 million closing.

But nothing could have prepared me for the disaster I walked into that night. The two guys running the show weren't just incompetent; they were complete buffoons. I had met them briefly at a Kenmare Christmas party, but I'd never had a real conversation with them. That dinner changed everything. They couldn't answer even the most basic questions about their own company, barely had a strategy in mind, and had no vision for the future. It was just blank stares and vague responses, at best. It was clear—this was going to be a problem. A big one.

The next morning, I arrived at Compact Video's headquarters—a sleek, modern three-story building just down the street from NBC Studios in Burbank. The place made a statement; across the rooftop, giant satellite dishes stood in perfect formation, angled toward the sky like they were listening for signals from deep space. On the inside, the company handled post-production services for Hollywood's biggest players—color correction, sound editing, and music layering. The kind of work that turned raw footage into something polished, seamless, and worthy of the big screen.

As I toured the facility, the Foley Room caught my attention. A cavernous space where sound editors recreated everyday noises—footsteps, creaking doors, breaking glass. Named after Jack Foley, the guy who pioneered the technique in the 1920s, the room was a playground for sound engineers. It had an endless supply of props, several flooring surfaces, and hidden tricks to make movie soundscapes feel real.

But beyond that fascinating corner of the business, everything else looked like something straight out of a NASA command center. The hazy and twilight-like lighting in the rooms, walls lined with flashing silver panels, joysticks, and glowing computer screens—it was a fortress of high-end tech. And yet, for all its cutting-edge equipment, this operation had a financial rot running straight to its core.

The first red flag for me was the two clueless executives I'd met at dinner the night before, who were obscenely overpaid. The president and CFO each pulled in a staggering $350,000 a year in base salary that was way above market. And they weren't the only ones cashing in. Across the board, salaries were inflated by at least 1.5 to 2 times what you'd expect in any other industry. The technicians, the real power players, had management wrapped around their fingers. Their routine was simple: demand a raise and the latest equipment, or walk over to a competitor who would give them both. And management always caved – *always.*

Then came the real kicker – the long-term lease on the building. The entire operation, packed with tens of millions of dollars in post-production equipment and pricey leasehold improvements, sat on shaky ground. Not to mention those massive satellite dishes on the roof. The landlord had all the leverage in the world. When the lease came up, negotiations would be a bloodbath. As if that wasn't bad enough, the constant need for new equipment devoured every dollar of depreciation that was supposed to contribute to free cash flow. In other words, the entire financial model was a fantasy. I ran the numbers and estimated cash losses at around $200,000 to $250,000 a month, with no way in sight to slash expenses enough to turn it around. Fixed costs were too high, capital expenditures were relentless, and debt service was crushing.

There was something else nagging at me. Manhattan Transfer, a later acquisition, looked suspiciously like a financial smoke screen. I couldn't prove it, but I'd seen enough creative bookkeeping over the years to recognize the smell of cooked balance sheets and income statements. "Purchase accounting" adjustments, when manipulated just right, could mask losses and artificially inflate asset values. It was the kind of trick that worked—until it didn't. Someone once told me, *"Liars figure, and figures lie."* I had a feeling that line applied here.

And the ones who would suffer would ultimately be the senior secured lenders, the unsecured debt holders, the shareholders, and, well, everyone. The company was bleeding out – it was known to all. The bank line of credit was nearly maxed, supplier payments were being stretched beyond terms, and our carried interests were officially underwater. I called Dan, who was already back in New York, and laid it all out. He was stunned at how deep the hole really was. But before I could even take a breath, he had another request.

"Can you swing by Phoenix on your way back? Take a look at Yellow Front."

I knew better than to say no.

If Compact Video was on life support, the senior secured lenders were the ones holding the oxygen mask. These were the big commercial banks—the ones that don't gamble unless the deck is stacked in their favor. They had the first line on everything that mattered, meaning if this ship went down, they got the lifeboats while everyone else fought for scraps.

Their money came in two forms: revolving credit lines and term loans. The revolving lines worked like a financial IV drip—borrow, repay, repeat, with interest due every month. But it wasn't a free-for-all. The amount they would actually lend was based on "eligible" assets. That meant only a portion of the company's accounts receivable (usually 70-85%) and inventory (up to 50%) counted. And not just any accounts receivable—past-due invoices and anything owed by the U.S. government were automatically excluded. (Yes, that's right. Banks don't trust the government to pay its bills, and for good reason.) Inventory was just as tricky. Anything old, obsolete, unsellable, or still in progress didn't make the cut.

Then there were the term loans, backed by hard assets—land, buildings, machinery, equipment, vehicles, furniture, leasehold improvements. Except, Compact Video didn't own the land or building, and it didn't have traditional manufacturing equipment. What did that leave? Some office furniture, fancy editing suites, and a pile of leasehold improvements that were basically worthless without a long-term lease. In a liquidation scenario, this wasn't collateral. It was junk.

The senior secured lenders had the best seat at the table, but it wasn't a comfortable one. Without a long-term lease, the whole operation was sitting on a time bomb. The moment the lease expired, everything inside the building—the expensive tech, the satellite dishes, the custom-built infrastructure—lost its value. And when banks smell risk, they start getting twitchy. Then there were the unsecured subordinated debt lenders—the adrenaline junkies of the finance world. They were the guys who played further down the food chain, knowing full well that if things went south, they'd be left holding the bag. "Subordinated" means exactly what it sounds like: they took a backseat to the secured lenders in any claim on the company's assets. Higher risk, higher reward—or so they hoped.

To make up for that risk, they charged steep interest rates, several points higher than the banks. But the real payday came from the warrants they got when the deal closed. These little golden tickets gave them the right to buy company stock for pennies on the dollar when things turned around. The goal? Cash in big when the company was sold or refinanced. If things went according to plan, they'd see a 25%+ annual return over five years. If things didn't go according to plan—well, that was someone else's problem.

In theory, it was a brilliant setup. In reality, Compact Video was already circling the drain. The senior secured lenders had collateral that wasn't worth much. The subordinated lenders were betting on a payday that would never come. And the shareholders? They were about to find out just how low "last in line" really was. This wasn't a company—it was a house of cards. And the wind was starting to blow.

If there's one universal truth in business, it's this: common shareholders eat last. When a company hits it big, they're the ones popping champagne. When it crashes, they're the ones sifting through the wreckage. That's just how the capital risk structure works. The banks and secured lenders get paid first, then the unsecured creditors, then—if there's anything left—the shareholders.

But here's the thrill: the upside is limitless. While lenders get back only what they're owed, common shareholders can make 10, 20, or even 100 times their original investment if the company skyrockets. When a business like Compact Video lands a massive buyout or goes public, debt holders get their cut, but the real winners are the shareholders who took the biggest risk. Their payday doesn't just repay their initial bet—it multiplies it. That's the kind of gamble Wall Street dreams are made of.

On the flip side, when a company sinks, shareholders are the first to lose everything. The secured lenders swoop in, selling off assets to recover their money. If there's anything left after that—and there usually isn't—it trickles down to unsecured creditors. And common shareholders, they get whatever scraps remain, which is often a big fat zero. Then there are the phantom stockholders—the ones holding carried interests. These people don't technically own stock, but their compensation is tied to the company's value. When the company wins, they win. When it collapses, their carried interest is worth as much as Monopoly money. No payout, no golden parachute.

Investing in a company like Compact Video wasn't for the faint of heart. It was a high-stakes game where a few walked away as legends while others were left explaining to their spouses why their net worth just evaporated. The winners wrote books and sat on panels. The losers went home with nothing but a hard lesson.

Yellow Front Stores had been snatched from Lucky Stores for $50 million, a bargain price for a $150 million business—if you ignored the fact that Lucky was fleeing the scene like a getaway driver. They were under siege by Asher B. Eshelman's hostile takeover bid, and with Wal-Mart's rapid expansion looming on the horizon, they saw the writing on the wall. Dumping Yellow Front was just a good survival strategy. Their massive Phoenix distribution facility was a fortress of white masonry, standing tall among palm trees, sharing a lobby with Checker Auto Parts. It looked the part—big, solid, and corporate. But looks can be deceiving.

Inside, I was ushered upstairs to meet the CEO, Bob Bove—a short, 50-something guy hiding under a tragic brown toupee. After some obligatory small talk, I cut to the chase. "What are your top strategic priorities?" His answer? "Finalizing the dress code."

I knew right then that this was going to be one hell of a visit.

Hoping for something more substantial, I turned to the CFO, who, to my amazement, looked exactly like Mickey

Mouse. And not just a little; the resemblance was uncanny. I asked for financials, only to discover that the January 1989 fiscal year-end statements—mind you, this was September—were nowhere to be found. No interim statements, and no operational reports. Nothing. How their lenders tolerated this level of incompetence was beyond me.

Still trying to salvage some useful insight, I was taken on a warehouse tour. That's when things went from bad to surreal. So, Mickey Mouse's CFO introduced me to the Operations Director, and I almost burst out laughing – it was his *twin!* There were two of them! I couldn't believe my eyes. All I could think was: Please let Mickey Mouse 2 be more competent than Mickey Mouse 1. And that hope lasted about 30 seconds.

We stepped into the massive 300,000-square-foot warehouse, and it was practically empty. Just vast, echoing aisles of bare pallet racks stretching from one end of the facility to the other. If you squinted, you could spot a few rubber boots and some fishing tackle. That was it. I asked how much inventory was supposed to be here. The answer: $25-30 million worth. But I was looking at maybe $5-10 million on a generous day. Mickey Mouse 2, unfazed, acted like this was business as usual. Then came the store visits. Bob Bove and I hit five or six locations across Phoenix, and at every one, it was about the same story. Half-empty shelves as far as the eye could see. It was obvious that the numbers didn't add up. Each store should have had around $250,000-$300,000 in inventory. Multiply that by 104 stores, and we were talking about tens of millions of dollars in missing stock. Add in the warehouse shortfall, and this wasn't just bad management; it was a full-blown crisis. Something was very, *very* wrong.

If Yellow Front was a sinking ship, then the Bonanza Stores, headquartered in Renton, Washington, acquisition several months later was like tying an anchor to a drowning man. The deal added 64 more locations and about $100 million in revenue, but let's be real—it was just lipstick on a pig, a subterfuge. Purchase accounting tricks had likely been used to mask the financial disaster that had started the moment Yellow Front changed hands. Just like with Compact Video, I didn't bother confronting anyone with my theory. The financials were so stale they were practically fossilized, and the business was too far gone to save. This operation was hemorrhaging cash, so much so that Compact Video, which had already been a financial dumpster fire, was starting to look like a decent investment in comparison. The same senior secured and unsecured subordinated debt lenders from Compact Video were back for round two, and they were about to get burned even worse. Another carried interest? Toast.

It took me less than two hours to assess the situation. I told Dan, in no uncertain terms, "This company is dead." There was no need for a post-mortem—assuming the Bonanza distribution centers and stores were in the same shape as Yellow Front (and I had zero doubt they were), it was only a matter of time before all 168 locations ran out of inventory completely. Dan didn't argue. Instead, he told me to stay put and hopped on a flight to Phoenix that Sunday.

That night, Dan met me for dinner at the hotel, bringing along a woman he'd met in Israel. She wasn't particularly attractive, didn't speak a word of English, and had absolutely nothing to contribute to our discussion about two failing businesses and the total incompetence of his team. To say the dinner was awkward would be an understatement.

By Monday morning, we sat down with Bob Bove and the CFO, two men who should have been dripping in shame but instead showed not a shred of embarrassment. No remorse, no accountability, just lost in the fog, and business as usual. That was when Dan made his move. He called in a turnaround specialist group from New York to assess the situation further, then asked me to babysit them. The company wired them $100,000 before they even got on the plane. I told Dan it was a colossal waste of money, but he did it anyway. I spent the next couple of days walking the specialists through the operation, pointing out the obvious:

no inventory, no financials, no future. By Saturday, I finally made it back to St. Louis, only to hop on a flight to New York the next evening. Monday morning, I sat down with Dan, Bob Silva, and Andy Mayer to lay out the ugly truth. Bob and Andy were stunned, to say the least.

And then, the real bombshell dropped. Despite everything, they decided both companies needed equity infusions. I told them they were absolutely out of their minds. But within days, they were knocking on the doors of their minority shareholders, trying to raise $5 million for each operation. Midland Group, a St. Louis-based real estate development firm brought in by Steve Trampe, held a stake in Compact Video. Overseas Partners, a private investment firm out of New York, had a stake in Yellow Front. And now, somehow, they were expected to throw good money after bad.

It was the textbook definition of denial.

While Compact Video and Yellow Front were locked in a desperate fight for survival, something even bigger was brewing behind the scenes. The management fees from these sinking operations were helping to prop up Kenmare's overhead, but that was about to come under the microscope. It was only a matter of time before the financial wreckage caught the attention of the minority shareholders, then the senior secured lender, and finally, the unsecured subordinated debt holder. This wasn't just a slow-motion train wreck. This was a financial time bomb, and the clock was ticking.

The equity infusions were a complete waste, and the cash burn was out of control. No amount of patchwork money was going to plug these holes—there would always be another cash call, another emergency, another crisis to bail out. And for what? A business model that was already six feet under. Take Compact Video, for example. Not having a long-term lease or an option to acquire the building—with all its expensive infrastructure and improvements—was one of the biggest screw-ups I'd ever seen in an acquisition. The fact that even the lenders missed this was beyond comprehension. But in the end, it wouldn't have mattered. The business itself was doomed from day one, and the seller knew it. They walked away clean while the new owners were left holding a ticking time bomb. That $5 million cash injection? It was already circling the drain.

Yellow Front was no different. The $5 million cash infusion there disappeared even faster—probably $1-2 million of it went straight into the pockets of those turnaround specialists, who spent months coming to the same conclusion I had in two hours. The plan to reorganize under Chapter 11 quickly turned into a conversation about Chapter 7 liquidation. The reality was clear: this wasn't a business that could be saved. It should have been put out of its misery the moment I set foot in that empty warehouse.

This is exactly why each acquisition had its own standalone legal entity. If it failed, you let it go. No emotion. No second chances. Just cut your losses and move on. That should have been the call with Yellow Front. Walking away on day one would have been the easiest business decision in history. But instead, people got sentimental, got stubborn, and threw good money after bad.

Thankfully, those of us with carried interests weren't dumb enough to sink our own cash into the mess. But that didn't mean we were untouched. The overall value of our carried interests across the Kenmare portfolio was shrinking fast. We weren't just watching one company go down—we were watching the foundation crack under the weight of bad deals, bad decisions, and bad luck.

The reckoning was coming.

On the bright side, the companies Bill and I had acquired and managed were still solid. They weren't flashy or the kind of businesses you'd brag about over cocktails, but they made money. Reliable, steady, predictable cash flow – the kind that makes financiers sleep easy at night.

But while our corner of the portfolio was humming along, the rest of Kenmare was heading straight for a cliff. 1

Madison Avenue was on edge. The portfolio Dan, Bob, and Andy had built was collapsing, and my sharp criticism of their management (or lack thereof) was starting to draw battle lines in the office. Needless to say, I was pissed. Their approach was nonchalant, bordering on reckless. They didn't manage their businesses. They collected success fees, slapped each other on the back, and then ran off chasing the next shiny deal. Meanwhile, their so-called "investments" were burning to the ground.

And honestly, what the hell were they thinking? Why were a bunch of financiers in New York running a 168-location retail chain in the western U.S.? Why were they pretending to know anything about a high-tech post-production company on the West Coast? Since when did Kenmare specialize in anything other than high-knowledge, low-tech manufacturing businesses—the kind we actually understood?

This wasn't just mismanagement. It was hubris. They thought they could play kingmakers, jumping from one deal to the next, while ignoring the mess they left behind. The cracks in the foundation weren't just from bad luck—they were from sheer neglect. And I wasn't about to sit back and watch the empire crumble. But it was clear that unless something changed fast, Kenmare was going to learn the hard way that arrogance is an expensive habit.

Chapter Seven: Gone Fishing

In early 1990, Dan pulled me into yet another mess, this time tied to his old boss and so-called mentor, Dr. Richard Gordon. Depending on who you asked, Gordon was either a brilliant scientist or a professional lunatic with too much money and not enough oversight. One of his claims to fame, if you believed the stories, was that he had formulated the chemical composition of Roundup for Monsanto. But instead of resting on that supposed achievement, he had taken his talents in a completely unrelated direction: running a catfish farm in the Arizona desert and shrimp trawlers in the South China Sea.

As bizarre as it sounded, that wasn't even the strangest part. The real irony was that one of his major investors was none other than one of the Simek brothers, the Wisconsin-based frozen pizza kingpins who had sold Tombstone Pizza to Kraft for a couple of hundred million dollars back in '86. After throwing piles of cash into the venture with nothing to show for it, Simek wanted out—fast. That's where Dan came in. And, unfortunately, I came in too.

A few months after my nightmare tour of Compact Video and Yellow Front, I found myself back in Arizona, this time staring at an operation so absurd it belonged in a parody of bad business decisions. We weren't talking about some modest, backyard fish farm. No, this was a full-blown industrial-scale endeavor, with an insane amount of water being pumped from deep beneath the desert floor—hundreds of thousands of gallons—just to keep these oversized mud-dwellers alive. The site was about 20 miles outside of Tempe, in the middle of nowhere, a forgotten patch of dust where Dr. Gordon had apparently decided to defy both logic and geography.

The setup was about as sophisticated as a kid's science project gone wrong. Large, rectangular pools stretched across the barren landscape, filled with sluggish catfish that looked just as confused about their location as I was. A single ramshackle building sat nearby, supposedly serving as the processing facility. "Processing" was a generous word. The place looked like it could barely function as a gas station, let alone a legitimate seafood operation.

Yet, somehow—somehow, the facility was passing inspections from regulatory authorities. I couldn't figure out if that was proof of their creativity in cutting corners or an indictment of the entire inspection system. Either way, it was clear that money was hemorrhaging from this operation at an alarming rate. Between the costs of pumping water, feeding the fish, and pretending this was a viable business, there was no possible way it could ever be profitable.

But Dr. Gordon didn't see it that way. He spoke about the farm with the kind of religious zeal usually reserved for cult leaders. He had convinced himself—and apparently Dan too—that this was the future of sustainable fish farming. He threw around phrases like "revolutionary aquaculture" and "vertical integration," as if jargon alone could turn this financial disaster into a goldmine.

I knew a lost cause when I saw one. And this wasn't just a lost cause—it was a first-place winner in the competition for dumbest business ventures ever conceived. I'd been sent to "look into the situation," but it didn't take more than a few hours to confirm what should have already been obvious: there was no situation to salvage. The only question was how much longer everyone was going to keep pretending otherwise.

Between the feed, water, utilities, payroll, insurance, and every other ridiculous expense you could imagine, the catfish farm and shrimp operation were chewing through around $20,000 a week. And for what? A miracle? A breakthrough in fish farming that would rewrite the rules of aquaculture? No. For a few sluggish catfish flopping around in desert pools and a couple of rusting shrimp trawlers stranded halfway across the world.

The revenue side of the ledger was an absolute joke. Every once in a while, they'd land a small sale, like the time Safeway bought $400 worth of catfish, and they'd celebrate like they had just closed a multimillion-dollar deal. But sales were rare, and excitement didn't pay the bills. The entire operation had been running for years before I arrived, and in all that time, they had barely generated enough revenue to cover a single week of expenses.

And then there was the shrimp situation, which was somehow even more absurd. The two trawlers, key assets in this so-called business, were sitting impounded by the Chinese police. Why? No one seemed to have a straight answer. Some vague, ominous mention of "legal complications" was all I got. So, in addition to the money pit in the desert, we now had a logistical nightmare in the South China Sea. And the best plan they had? Figuring out how to sweet-talk the Chinese authorities into letting the boats go.

I called Dan, laid everything out for him, and expected some kind of rational response, and maybe even an ounce of the business sense he once had. But instead of acknowledging that we were looking at a dead-end venture with no hope of profitability, he doubled down. He wanted to help out his old mentor, Dr. Gordon. His plan was for Kenmare to step in and split the weekly financial burden with the original investor group.

I couldn't believe what I was hearing. I told him straight up: "Dan, this will never, *never*, be cash flow positive. Not in our lifetimes, not in anyone's lifetime." But it didn't matter. He was locked in. Against my outright pleadings, Kenmare started writing the checks. And while we were beginning to start lighting our money on fire by funding half of this farce, the original investors were happy to throttle back on their contributions as Dan foolishly inserted himself into the mix.

Returning to Phoenix and checking into the Arizona Biltmore Hotel brought back a vivid memory from a business trip years ago that happened to coincide with an NFL owners' meeting. The hotel was packed with NFL owners, coaches, media personalities, you name it. For a football fan like me, it was a fascinating scene.

At one point during my stay, I found myself a little too close—literally—to one of the biggest and most recognizable figures in the entire league.

I was walking through the lobby when I noticed Joe Robbie, the principal founder of the Miami Dolphins, being interviewed live for a radio broadcast near the front windows. Curious, I glanced in that direction for just a few seconds while continuing to walk. Then, *boom*.

I turned my head just in time to plant my face squarely into the chest of a towering 6'3" man. And not just any man—Mike Ditka. Yes, *that* Mike Ditka. At the time, he was the head coach of the Chicago Bears and already a Hall of Fame player and legendary football figure.

It was one of those moments when time slows down from sheer embarrassment. I wasn't sure who was more surprised, but I absolutely knew who was more mortified. I started apologizing profusely, practically tripping over my own words. To his credit, Ditka could not have been more gracious. He just chuckled, brushed off his chest, and gave me a quick nod before continuing on his way.

We both walked off in opposite directions, he probably wondering who the clueless guy was that body-checked him in the middle of the Biltmore lobby, and I wondering how

I'd just turned a casual stroll into a shoulder-level collision with an NFL icon.

By the time April 1990 rolled around, I was headed to Rockport, Massachusetts, for a board meeting at Dr. Gordon's summer house. The goal was to sit down with my counterpart from the original investor group and somehow hash out a plan to "move forward together." Whatever that meant.

But by this point, I wasn't just questioning the sanity of the business, I was questioning Dan's. It was as if he had undergone some kind of financial lobotomy. This was the same man who had built his reputation on a brutally simple motto: *"It's just as important not to lose money as it is to make money."*

Well, that motto had apparently packed its bags and left the building. Along with any sense of financial discipline, Dan once had. And I was left sitting in the wreckage, trying to make sense of it all.

At the very least, I figured Rockport would be a nice setting for a board meeting. I'd never been, but I imagined a charming coastal town, fresh ocean air, and maybe even a good meal to take the edge off the absurdity of this entire operation. I was wrong. The house where we were meeting was a single-story shack with a maroon exterior and white window frames, and it looked like it hadn't been touched since the 1920s. Or cleaned since the 1950s. The paint was peeling, the windows were clouded with grime, and the whole place reeked of mildew and neglect. Inside, it was worse. A thick, musty stench hung in the air like a curse, the kind that settles into the walls and refuses to leave.

Dr. Gordon had promised us a grand lobster feast, which sounded great at the time. But when we arrived, we realized he meant *just* lobster. No sides, no appetizers, and the most atrocious offence: no *butter*. Not even bread or a damn lemon wedge. Just piles of lobster dumped on the table, accompanied by a roll of paper towels. It was a meal only a starving castaway could appreciate.

I made the mistake of checking the fridge, hoping for *something* to balance out the shellfish buffet. Big mistake. Inside was a graveyard of forgotten condiments, half-empty bottles of mystery sauces, and a single rusted can of beer that looked like it had been sitting there since Nixon was in office.

That night, I had every intention of toughing it out and getting some sleep, but between the stiff, ancient mattress and the air that was stuffy with mold spores, it was impossible. By morning, my sinuses felt like they had been invaded by whatever was growing in that house. The shower was a horror show—black mold climbing the walls like ivy, the smell of damp rot so strong it nearly turned my stomach.

The next morning for breakfast, I don't know what I expected. There was just some bad coffee. No milk, no cream, not even a sugar packet in sight. I choked down half a cup and prayed my stomach wouldn't turn on me after the questionable seafood from the night before. But as miserable as the whole experience was, I did manage to pull off one small victory that day.

During the meeting, there was a full-court press to assign *me* as the point man for resolving the shrimp trawler fiasco in China. Apparently, they figured since I was the new guy on the board, I should be the one to fly across the world and deal with foreign law enforcement. I saw that trap a mile away and dodged it. Instead, I successfully pawned it off on one of Dr. Gordon's die-hard followers from the catfish farm. If he was so committed to the cause, let him wade through the bureaucratic nightmare and try his luck with the Chinese police.

Dan, still clinging to whatever misguided sense of loyalty he had to Gordon, agreed to continue funding this disaster, splitting the costs with the original investors. And so, for another four months, we kept shoveling money into the furnace, watching it go up in smoke.

Finally, after months of fighting a battle that should never have been fought, my counterpart and I convinced them to let it go. The trawlers weren't coming back, and the farm was a money pit; there was no miracle waiting around the corner. It took longer than it should have, 4 months to be exact, but in the end, even Dan had to admit defeat.

Chapter Eight: Game-Changing

It was the Monday of Labor Day weekend, 1990, and I had just landed back in New York, ready to start what I thought would be a routine workweek. The city was still sticky with the late-summer heat, and the lull of the holiday made Monday feel deceptively calm, and enough so to mask the storm that was about to hit.

By Tuesday morning, it was clear something was amiss. Andy, our Controller, looked worse than usual. He'd been struggling with stomach issues for months – pretty much since Compact Video and Yellow Front went up in flames. The stress was clearly eating him alive. The guy was in his early thirties, like me, but he looked ten years older. His pale face and tight-lipped silences told you more than any doctor could. Hell, at one point, he even told me he'd been coughing up blood, and I suspected an ulcer. Now I knew why.

Part of Andy's stress was tied to his double role: not just my colleague, but the man juggling Kenmare's entire financial structure. And with our two revenue engines—Compact and Yellow Front—officially dead in the water, Andy was left to figure out how to keep the lights on without the management fees that had been covering our hefty overhead.

On Wednesday, September 5th, I flew out of LaGuardia and headed to Chicago for a scheduled meeting with our investment bankers at Rodman & Renshaw. The flight was smooth, the sky clear, and as soon as I landed, I called the New York office from the terminal to check in with Lynn, the administrative assistant I shared with Dan. Lynn was primarily responsible for answering incoming calls and everything else, and she always kept our world spinning smoothly.

She rattled off a few routine messages, but one stopped me cold. A call had come in from the audit team at Baird, Kurtz & Dobson—the CPAs handling Detroit Tool's audit and tax work. They were waiting on some simple bank balance confirmations from Andy so they could close out Detroit Tool's July 1990 fiscal year audit; it was easy stuff, or so I thought. I then had Lynn transfer me over to Andy to check on the delay. I also figured I'd give him a quick update on the Shannon Group deal, which we were in talks to sell to a Florida-based private equity firm called Trivest. The deal was shaky at best, and I figured Andy would want the latest.

But before I could get into any of that, Andy said something that knocked the air right out of me.

"I need to tell you something," he told me. "The Detroit Tool audit is going to be a problem. There aren't going to be any bank confirmations. Dan took the money."

At first, I thought I had misheard. "What?" I asked urgently.

He repeated it, even slower this time, "Dan. Took. The. Money."

I remained calm, and all I did was ask Andy if Dan was in the office so that I could speak with him, but he wasn't – typical. I told Andy to hang tight and that I was getting on the next flight back to New York. I didn't know what exactly I was walking into, but I knew the situation could not be good. So, I decided that I would cancel the meeting with Rodman & Renshaw on the spot and return immediately to New York.

A few hours later, I was back at LaGuardia and didn't even stop to catch my breath. It was just straight into a cab, and right to 1 Madison Avenue. By the time I got there, it was mid-afternoon. The adrenaline was coursing through my veins as I stepped off the elevator expecting to find Dan sitting in his corner office, waiting for me with some kind of explanation—or at least a half-baked cover story. But no, he was gone.

Turns out, after getting a "heads-up" call from Andy, Dan had made an abrupt decision to fly to London for a *"long weekend."* The timing was about as subtle as a brick through a window.

The energy in the office was unusually quiet; not your typical midweek buzz. The senior team—Bill, Bob, and Andy—were all avoiding eye contact with the younger staff. It didn't take a genius to realize something was terribly wrong. After Dan fled, Andy had filled Bill and Bob in on what had happened—my call, the missing Detroit Tool funds, and the ticking time bomb that was now sitting squarely in our collective laps.

The rest of the office, though, was still blissfully unaware.

Our admin team—Lynn, Helene, and Rose—kept their usual rhythm going, typing away and fielding calls like nothing had changed. The analysts—Robert Salisbury, Jeff Gerstell, and Matt Barry—were all heads down, modeling deals that probably didn't have a future anymore. There was something almost tragic about watching them work so hard, not knowing the foundation was already cracked beneath their feet.

And then there was Andy; people weren't exactly mad at him. The sentiment was more akin to disappointment. But not mad. No one could ignore the hold Dan had over certain people. I've said it before—Dan had a strange sort of power. Not charisma, exactly, but more like control. He had this eerie ability to make smart, reasonable people act against their better judgment. There was something *Dracula-esque* about it, and Andy had clearly been bitten. Whatever secrets Dan carried, he'd made sure others were too scared or too loyal, or too compromised, to speak up.

Andy wasn't just a colleague; he was a peer. We all were. Andy, Bob, Bill, and I each reported directly to Dan, so we shared the same weight on our shoulders, the same late-night calls, the same endless dance with risk. In that kind of environment, trust isn't optional; it's the whole game. Bob, Bill, and I agreed: we needed to regroup. This wasn't the kind of thing you solve in a conference room or over another stale cup of office coffee. We needed space and perspective, and a stiff drink or two wouldn't hurt either.

So that evening, the three of us made our way to Piccolo Mondo, our go-to spot away from the chaos. It had become our unofficial war room over the years—a place where deals were celebrated, tensions eased, and where things needed to be said if they were off the record. Bill and I kept to our rhythm; it was our go-to time. For Bob, though, this was a detour. He lived out in Morristown, New Jersey, with a long train ride typically waiting for him after work. But tonight, that would have to wait. The stakes were too high, and the fallout from the day was just beginning to sink in.

We didn't waste time with small talk. The moment the car pulled away from 1 Madison, it was all about one thing: *The Problem*. That's how we referred to it, capitalized, singular, and ominous. We all knew we needed Dan to come clean and face the accusations so that he could help us find a way out. But it didn't take long to see the cracks forming between us. There was a very real difference in urgency between what I felt and what they were ready to do.

That's when I first saw it—Bill's loyalty to Dan was immovable. Logic, ethics, even legality—all of it took a back seat to the bond they had. Decades of deals, close calls, and wins had built something hard to challenge. Even now, with everything on fire, Bill's instinct wasn't to extinguish it, and all of it was to protect Dan from the blaze. That moment, subtle as it was, marked the beginning of the end for what I once believed was a solid friendship.

Bob, on the other hand, wasn't driven by loyalty. He was driven by practical and personal fear. He had a new wife, a house in the suburbs, and—God help him—brand new triplets from his third marriage. His focus wasn't on Detroit Tool or integrity or moral consequences. All he wanted was a steady income and a fragile domestic balance. And honestly, I couldn't blame him.

But neither of them had the same skin in the game that I did. Bill and Bob weren't officers or directors of Detroit Tool. They didn't have relationships with the stakeholders, the lenders, or the Missouri-based minority shareholders, many of whom had ties to Compact Video. They weren't responsible for the livelihoods of 400 employees, but I was; I had real, legal, and moral accountability. And beyond that, I cared.

Sure, I didn't have decades of history with Dan. And yeah, my wife was pregnant with our first child, due in January 1991. But I had a low overhead, both financially and emotionally, with no obligations that blurred my judgment or any blind loyalties. Just a clear line of sight to what was right and what had gone very, very wrong.

The evening didn't turn hostile, but by the time the last Sambuca hit the table and our two black service cars pulled up outside, the writing was on the wall—reaching any kind of consensus about how to handle the Problem, whether the next day or after Dan returned from his little adventure in London, was going to be an uphill battle. The only real point of agreement we landed on was this: instead of cornering Andy as a group, I'd sit down with him one-on-one the next day to see what he knew about Dan and the disappearing cash. But the ride home with Bill was awkward, and we barely spoke. That silence said more than words could have, and none of it sat right with me.

Something had shifted, and there would be no going back.

Every Kenmare portfolio company followed the same playbook when it came to cash control. Detroit Tool—or more accurately, the cluster of companies under that name—was no exception. As part of standard procedure, we opened duplicate sets of operating bank accounts: one in the community where the business operated, and another right downstairs at the Chase Manhattan Bank on the first floor of our building at 1 Madison Avenue. One for local use, one for our watchful eyes in New York.

The person overseeing a company—me, in Detroit Tool's case—was responsible for setting up the Chase accounts. Alongside me, the authorized signers were always the same: Andy, wearing his dual hat as Kenmare's controller, and of course, Dan. At the local level, it was a mix of operational staff, and, again, it was Andy, Dan, and me. It was a system built to ensure control, transparency, and fluid movement of capital. The rules were simple: any cash beyond a set local threshold was routinely swept into the Chase account in New York. If you needed money on the ground, you had to put in a request, and it would be transferred back as needed. It kept things clean and ensured accountability. Or it did in theory, anyway.

By July 31, 1990—barely a year after we closed on Detroit Tool—we should've been sitting on around $15 million in total cash across all those accounts. Most of it was supposed to be tucked away safely in our Chase accounts. That was the plan. But plans, as I was quickly learning, don't matter when the people executing them go rogue.

The Thursday after our uneasy dinner at Piccolo Mondo, Bill had left our apartment early. He walked to the office alone for the first time in years. That morning, when I stepped into our shared office at 1 Madison, I felt it right away; it was a certain chill in the air, and it certainly wasn't the air-conditioning.

But we didn't say much. Bill had buried himself in papers, and I dove back into work too, but my mind was split. Before the Problem had exploded, my biggest project was the sale of The Shannon Group—the walk-in and reach-in refrigeration outfit we'd built from scratch. I loved that business, and I know Bill did too. We weren't ready to sell it off, not yet.

The Welbilt acquisition in California, which we folded into the group not long ago, was just starting to show its potential. Give it another few years, and we could have pulled an extra $10 to $15 million out of the final price tag. At the time, market multiples for a $100 million revenue company were floating in the six-to-seven times EBITDA range. Every additional million in earnings was worth its weight in gold.

We had just completed major capital improvements, synchronized production tooling across all plants, and were finally positioned to rake in free cash flow. It felt criminal to sell now. Still, Dan had pushed for it. We brought on Bowles Hollowell Conner & Co. out of Charlotte as our investment bankers in June, and I was knee-deep with them every day. Packaging financials and prepping pitch materials—Thursday was no different.

But as I sat there, putting together yet another buyer profile, something gnawed at me: Why now? Why sell a cash cow just before it explodes? Then it hit me. Maybe this wasn't about timing, but rather about *cover*. If Dan had been quietly draining Detroit Tool, the Shannon Group sale was his exit strategy. Maybe he planned to patch the missing millions with fresh proceeds. But then again, the audit for Detroit Tool was for the fiscal period that ended in July, so that angle didn't line up.

Still, the idea lingered. Because when the numbers stop adding up, everything starts to look like a motive.

Andy strolled into 1 Madison a little after 9:00 a.m. that morning, fresh off the New Jersey Transit and looking like a man whose secret had just been dragged out into the daylight, relieved, but still wrecked inside. We met in his office an hour later, and now, there was no pretending and no skirting around what we both knew. We had always worked well together; no frills and no ego, just good chemistry. Though we never hung out after hours, I'd still have called him a friend. And right then, it felt like two friends facing down the same monster in the dark. He had a young family—a wife and a couple of toddlers. I could see the weight of that in his eyes. Whatever Dan had roped him into, Andy was now deep in it, and the cost wasn't just numbers in a ledger. It was his name, his career, maybe his freedom.

He exhaled, leaned back in his chair, and started talking.

Andy confirmed what I had suspected: Dan had been funneling cash from the Detroit Tool accounts to fund personal projects. It was no investments or ventures, just sinking ships and vanity plays. He used part of the money—Andy guessed around $3 to $5 million—to cover his share of cash calls for Yellow Front and Compact Video. That was two companies already circling the drain. Dan knew that money was never coming back; he had to have known. It was like watching someone throw bricks into a black hole and hoping to build a house on the other side. But it didn't stop there.

Andy estimated another $2 to $3 million went into a new co-op apartment Dan was outfitting in Tribeca with custom finishes and the top-floor unit. But it was discreet, of course. No one in the office even knew he was moving; he kept it on the down-low, like a man building a bunker, or a bolt-hole. Then came his divorce. That reportedly cost another $1 to $2 million in cash as part of the settlement. That brought the known tally to somewhere between $6 and $10 million.

And then Andy stopped talking.

"What about the rest?" I asked.

He looked down and fidgeted with a pen. Then there was a pause, which was the worst part. Somewhere between $5 to $9 million was just gone. Poof; no record or explanation, just a void.

I thanked him, told him we'd figure it out, and left his office feeling like I'd just watched a house burn in slow motion. Later that day, Bill took off for his place on Cape Cod. He didn't say much before he left, but he didn't need to. Normally, he would remain in New York until late Friday morning, but not this time. And somehow, that small break from routine screamed louder than words.

By Friday afternoon, I was done too. I caught an earlier flight to St. Louis, my head spinning, and my stomach twisted. The weekend wasn't restful in the slightest. How could it be? I had all the pieces, but they weren't fitting together. I didn't tell anyone what I'd learned and figured that I owed Dan one last chance to explain himself before making moves, mano a mano.

I flew back into New York on Sunday night, September 9th, but Bill didn't and waited until Monday morning to return from Hyannis. That wasn't off-kilter on paper, but it felt off, like Thursday's early departure and like the way he hadn't looked me in the eye since Piccolo Mondo. Things were changing, gradually and quietly, and not in a good way.

Dan was due back soon. And when he walked in, everything—friendship, loyalty, power—was going to be tested.

Chapter Nine: What Now?

The office was offbeat on Monday and Tuesday—too quiet in some ways and too careful in others. Bill, Andy, and Bob all seemed to be walking on eggshells. You could feel it in the hallway glances, the clandestine side conversations, the way their body language screamed one thing: *Keep your guard up.* Everyone was pretending to be focused on the day-to-day, but under the surface, we were just orbiting one central question: What the hell would happen now?

By Wednesday, the temperature had risen—not the weather outside, but the mood inside. That morning, I was called into Dan's office for an 11 a.m. meeting, just me and him. No one else. That alone was rare enough to raise eyebrows since Dan didn't do many solo, closed-door meetings. His corner office was more like a showroom of power—wide open, windows on both sides, modern art, and Lucite deal tombstones displayed like trophies. Most meetings happened informally, on the sectional couch across from his desk. The couch was flanked by a coffee table with fresh-cut flowers and an embroidered pillow that read: *"Happiness is a Positive Cash Flow."* A smug little mantra, sure—but one that usually made sense around here.

Not today.

Dan didn't motion to the couch, he pointed toward one of the stiff-backed chairs in front of his desk. The move was deliberate, maybe even theatrical. No coffee, small talk, or welcome. Just a seat across from the man whose fingerprints were now all over the most serious problem Kenmare had ever faced. My instincts kicked in; I knew this wasn't going to be a friendly check-in. This was something else—something more primal.

I'd never had a real confrontation with Dan in the entire time I spent with him. Sure, we'd disagreed on deal terms here and there—he liked to tinker late in the game, and sometimes it drove me nuts, but I chalked it up to his style. Sometimes, his last-minute changes even made things better. They were strategic tweaks, not personal ones. I respected his brain, even if I didn't always trust his methods. In my bones, I felt that this was a different ballgame altogether. This was personal, financial, and wrong on so many levels.

Up until now, I'd given Dan the benefit of the doubt. He wasn't warm like Bill, and we weren't close outside of work, but he was smart, driven, and generally seemed to know how to win. That was enough to keep the machine running. But now, that same drive to win had turned toxic. The charm was gone; the mask was off. And I had questions—serious ones.

Loyalty was shifting. The things I thought were unshakeable—trust, structure, leadership—were now sitting on wobbly ground. I had a front-row seat to something dangerous, and I wasn't sure how far Dan was willing to go to keep the illusion alive.

What I did know was this: I was no longer just a rising executive at Kenmare. I was a witness, maybe even a liability. And I was about to learn how Dan operated when cornered. This wasn't going to be business as usual.

The whole time, Dan didn't blink or break a sweat. He sat behind that glossy desk and confirmed everything Andy had told me—every dollar, every misstep, every single one of the jaw-dropping transfers from Detroit Tool to Kenmare. His delivery was casual, almost smug, like he was discussing line items on a lunch tab. Then came his personal brand of delusion.

"They're in Kenmare CDs," he said, completely straight-faced. "Certificates of Deposit."

That was the moment I realized that something here was rotten to the core. Not just financially, but mentally. I thought of Lynn—our trusted, no-nonsense admin—and what she had let slip to me over coffee a few weeks back. She said Dan was seeing not one, but *two* therapists. At the time, I brushed it off. New York execs and shrinks go together like espresso and stress. But now? Now I was thinking maybe he needed a third. Or at least a full-time reality check.

Dan was calm, almost disturbingly so, as he explained that the transfers Andy executed were within his authority. No regrets or second thoughts. Not even an acknowledgment of the chaos he had unleashed. He had no plan to reverse them, not in the slightest. I was stunned, but I held my posture and pushed back.

"Dan, this violates the loan covenants with Westinghouse Credit. You know that," I said. "You're also breaching the Shareholders Agreement with Midland Group."

He didn't care; his indifference was surgical. There was no concern about the lender or any mention of Midland's senior management team. Hell, not even a grasp of the potential legal, financial, and reputational damage spiraling toward us like a freight train. Instead, he took a different angle.

"Frankly," he said, "I'm starting to question your loyalty to the firm."

My loyalty? The man was gambling with company funds like he was moving poker chips at a casino, and he was questioning *my* loyalty?

He leaned back, narrowed his eyes, and warned that if I said anything to Westinghouse, to Midland, to anyone, it might damage *his* "career."

Career. It wasn't just tone-deaf, it was a surreal misread of the stakes. We weren't talking about a bruised résumé; we were staring down the barrel of a potential financial disaster. This wasn't about bad press or wounded pride. It was about the health of a business, the integrity of leadership, and people's livelihoods.

I tried one last angle. "Then let's figure out a plan," I said. "Let's talk about a way to return the money to Detroit Tool, even if it's in phases."

He wasn't having it; he left no room for discussion or compromise. Just that same eerie calm. That kind of certainty isn't strength, it's delusion dressed up as confidence.

I left his office in a fog. I wasn't angry, I was just stunned. Everything I thought I understood about Dan—the ambition, the control, the instincts was crumbling. This wasn't a moment of lapse in judgment; it was a calculated risk that reeked of self-preservation, not leadership.

Walking back to my desk, I couldn't stop thinking, *questioning my loyalty to the firm. Wow!* That phrase just echoed in my head. Because that was the moment I knew—Dan wasn't looking for a way out of the mess. He was preparing to survive it. And he didn't care who got taken down in the process.

And now, whether I liked it or not, I was part of the story.

I spent the rest of that Wednesday buried in work. No choice, really. There were still deals to close, reports to finalize, and questions to answer. The Shannon Group sale to Trivest was entering its final stretch, and our investment bankers at Bowles Hollowell Conner & Co. needed a steady stream of updated financials, clean admin reports, and crisp summaries. So, I kept my head down, banging out the deliverables like a man trying to outrun a fire—and in some ways, I was.

But even as I pushed through the numbers and dotted every "i" and crossed every "t", my mind kept drifting back to *the Problem*. The transfers. Dan's indifference. His psychotic calm. That ridiculous talk of "Kenmare CDs." None of it was going away. And doing nothing? That was never on the table—not for me.

If Dan wouldn't listen to reason, I needed to bring in someone he *would* listen to. Someone with history. Someone with leverage. That someone, I figured, was Steve Trampe.

Steve wasn't just any old associate; he was Dan's longtime partner in the Cordage Mill real estate deals in St. Louis and the man who brought Midland Group into the Detroit Tool investment in the first place. His involvement gave the whole deal credibility from day one. On top of that, he had a seat on Detroit Tool's board. His influence was more than just personal; it was structural.

I'd worked with Steve back in the Mark Twain days, and we had a solid and respectful relationship. He knew me well enough to trust my judgment. He also knew I wasn't a drama starter; I was raising red flags, but it wasn't for effect. It was because something was *truly* wrong.

So, I picked up the phone and I laid it out for him—everything I had uncovered, everything Dan had confirmed, and every step Andy took along the way. I didn't sugarcoat any of it. And thankfully, I didn't need to. Steve caught my drift immediately. He wasn't shocked, exactly, but he was clearly disturbed. The trust he had in Dan as a business partner was on thin ice. And the respect was starting to erode. Like me, Steve had one goal in mind—to protect Detroit Tool. He knew the company was a solid play with a huge upside. It just needed to stay clean, and this mess was the opposite of clean.

Steve told me he was getting on the next flight to New York, without missing a beat. The next day, Thursday, we were back in Dan's office. This time it was me and Steve in those two formal chairs across from Dan's desk—not lounging on the sectional, not smiling over coffee. It wasn't a friendly check-in; it was an intervention.

Steve didn't waste time. He came in composed but serious, armed with the facts I had given him and that Midwestern firmness that didn't need raised voices to pack a punch. He asked Dan straight up to walk him through the transfers—how they were justified, how they aligned with the loan covenants, and how the minority shareholders were being protected.

Dan tried to hold his ground. But this wasn't just me sitting across from him anymore—this was his old friend, his partner, someone who knew exactly what had been built and how easily it could unravel. Watching Dan squirm under Steve's questions was like watching a con man try to bluff with a losing hand. And still, Dan stayed defiant. He kept his cool, yes. But unbending.

That meeting marked the moment I realized we weren't just dealing with a financial issue. We were staring at a bigger breakdown—a fracture in leadership, a breach of trust, and maybe even a slow-motion collapse. If Steve couldn't pull Dan back to reality, then the situation was worse than I thought, much worse.

Dan, however, doubled down. Sitting there with Steve and me across from him, he calmly—and almost absurdly—reaffirmed everything: the transfers, the so-called "Kenmare CDs," and his absolute refusal to commit to any plan that would return the funds to Detroit Tool. It was frustrating and surreal.

You'd think the presence of Steve—his longtime partner, someone with skin in the game—might get him to sing like a canary. Maybe shake loose a little logic, but no. Dan stayed rooted in his fantasy that this sleight-of-hand with Detroit Tool's cash was perfectly legitimate. He wasn't budging. Not an inch.

Steve and I walked out of that office, exchanging looks of complete disbelief. Bewildered was an understatement. This wasn't just an executive misstep anymore—it was a full-blown leadership crisis. One that could put an entire company, its board, its shareholders, and everyone else involved in serious jeopardy.

We needed leverage. Real leverage. And fast.

So, right there, standing in the hallway outside Dan's office, we made the call. We told him plainly that we were going to call a meeting of the board of directors of the parent company, *Detroit Tool Group, Inc.,* on Monday, October 8th. That gave us three weeks—just enough time to prepare a clear-eyed summary of the facts and start pushing toward a resolution. Or, at the very least, force Dan to face some hard truths with a full board looking on.

I flew back to St. Louis that Friday, September 14th, a bit earlier than usual since I needed the time. And I needed the distance from New York. By the time I touched down, Steve and I already had a plan in motion. That same evening, we sat down to draft a formal notice of the upcoming board meeting, keeping it simple and clean, with no hint of what was coming or a detailed agenda. We intended for it to be a quiet little bomb with a timestamp: October 8th. Held in St. Louis. Attendance expected.

It was Friday afternoon when the notices went out to each board member. Now, you might think sending out a board meeting notice without disclosing the elephant in the room was playing it a little too close to the vest. But this wasn't about creating panic, it was about setting the stage—carefully and strategically. The last thing we wanted was back-channel drama or Dan trying to poison the well before we could speak the truth in a structured setting. This had to happen face-to-face and in broad daylight.

And frankly, we didn't want to give Dan time to manipulate the narrative. He was too good at that; too comfortable in chaos. We needed the element of surprise, and more importantly, we needed to make sure the *board* heard the story before the spin could start.

I remember sitting at home that night, staring at the TV, but not paying much attention. It felt a little like loading a chamber and setting a countdown clock at the same time. Three weeks was all we had. Now, the line had been drawn, and we had to brace for whatever came next.

Chapter Ten: Meet Me in St. Louis

The notice had been sent, and the date was set. October 8th was supposed to be the day everything came to a head. But nothing ever runs on time when people start feeling the heat.

On September 21st, a response came in from the Midland Group, saying that they couldn't make it—Columbus Day weekend, people were traveling. A few carefully worded sentences later, the board meeting was pushed to October 15th. Delay by default. The kind of delay that carries tension in its silence.

In the meantime, things got... weird.

Inside the office, the temperature dropped without anyone touching the thermostat. People kept it professional, but distant. Bill and I, once joined at the hip in both hustle and history, mostly avoided the elephant in the room. We'd let our guard down only after-hours, over drinks and dinner at Piccolo Mondo. Even then, the conversation had the weight of a confession whispered behind closed church doors.

Steve and I weren't sitting on our hands. We threw ideas at Dan like lifelines—logical, strategic, even generous ones. Sell Kenmare's majority stake in Detroit Tool for $8 million. Or maybe just buy out Midland Group's minority interest for $5 million. If that was too bold, fine—how about a simple pledge? We offered to allocate $1.2 million from the upcoming sale of The Shannon Group to show Midland we were trying to make it right.

Dan's reaction was somewhere between glazed and ghosted. He wasn't angry or resistant; he was just absent and disconnected. The man who once had the drive and cunning to pull deals out of thin air now looked like someone quietly slipping off the edge of his own narrative. Amid all of this, I had a brief escape. My younger sister got married in late September, in a charming bed-and-breakfast tucked in the woods outside Hartford. I was a groomsman, surrounded by family and joy in the crisp autumn with my pregnant wife by my side. Everyone was smiling, and no one had a clue. It was the perfect wedding weekend for them.

I, on the other hand, smiled through it. But in the back of my head, I couldn't stop thinking, *If they only knew...*

Then came October 10th, an absolute circus of a day. Dan and I boarded a flight to Pittsburgh for a face-to-face with Westinghouse Credit. The plan was to dazzle them with a smoke-and-mirrors pitch that involved buying out Midland Group, paying a one-time dividend, and sweetening the pot by selling off Detroit Tool Metal Products Co.

Westinghouse's reaction was priceless: *You want to do what?*

They didn't laugh, but they didn't bite either. Instead, they asked us to come back with a formal plan and detailed projections. A polite way of saying, *You better be serious, or don't come back at all.*

I walked out of that meeting knowing one thing: I had to get ahead of this, and I had to do it fast. If I didn't tell Westinghouse the truth soon, I'd end up holding the same bag of bad decisions and wearing the same stink. That night, Dan and I flew back to New York. Steve Trampe joined us for dinner, and we went over the Westinghouse meeting. Dan had no plan or path forward. Nothing had changed.

Then he asked to delay the board meeting again, which we refused. *Tick-tock.* We had five days left.

The morning of Monday, October 15th, arrived like a freight train. At exactly 10:00 AM, the board gathered inside the Cordage Mill Development office—an old industrial building converted into a crisp, modern space. The conference room sat just off the main office bullpen area. Every single board member was present, including the Midland Group guys, whom I had never met in person before, Jim Murtha, Lee Wielansky, and even Ken Goldberg, the so-called "Advisory Director" who had no legal vote, pulled up a chair. But before we could even convene the meeting, Dan dropped his first card on the table.

He declared, in his usual smug calm, that *this wasn't an official board meeting.* His reasoning? As Chairman, he alone had the authority to call a special meeting under the Articles of Incorporation and Bylaws of Detroit Tool Group, Inc., and since he didn't call this one—well, technically, it didn't count. The room was dead quiet for a beat. Not stunned, exactly, just baffled.

Then, Dan shifted gears and gestured to Dave Wessell. As President of both Detroit Tool operating companies, Dave was the only person full-time on site running the day-to-day business with clarity and calm, and Dan asked him to give an update on operations in Lebanon, Missouri. Dave looked confused but delivered. His report was steady, focused, and practical; an anchor in a meeting drifting quickly into absurdity.

But no sooner had Dave wrapped up than Dan told him there was no need for him to stick around. His words were polite, but the message was clear: *You're not invited to the real conversation.* Dave, still visibly confused, left the building and headed back to Lebanon, two hours away down Highway 44 and worlds away from the storm brewing in that room.

Afterward, Jim Murtha casually let it slip that he and Lee Wielansky had met with Dan the day before. Dan had already told them about the so-called "$5 to $9 million investment." Apparently, Dan had also decided that Dave Wessell shouldn't know about it, *for now.*

Steve and I weren't shocked. Dan liked to inoculate people privately, drip by drip. Control the story, control the fallout. Honestly, in this case, we didn't disagree. As much as we respected Dave, dragging him into this mess now would only distract him from running the business, which, ironically, was one of the few things still working. Dan then pulled out a letter from Alan Jacobs, a long-time attorney for Dan, his previous investment group, Kenmare, and its portfolio companies, including Detroit Tool, backing up his claim that only the Chairman could call a formal board meeting. It was a legal technicality, sure, but one that gave Dan more cover than he deserved.

Steve and I pressed for the board to retain independent counsel—someone not tangled up in this mess, and someone who could speak for the board itself.

Dan declined; no big surprise there. He *did* agree, however, to set up a meeting with Alan Jacobs and a limited number of members of the board. Classic Dan: offer just enough to stall.

Not long after, Dan left for the airport, New York-bound, leaving behind more questions than answers, and still *nothing* on the official corporate record about the Problem. That same afternoon, Steve and I drafted a letter to Dan, pushing back. We formally requested that he call a real, official board meeting to discuss the allegations and open the door to a proper investigation. No more dodging; it was time to get this on the books.

That infamous "$5 to $9 million investment" Dan kept tossing around like a poker chip? My read on it was blunt: the full $9 million was long gone, burned through and scattered across Andy's list of greatest hits—Compact Video capital calls, Yellow Front disasters, the sleek Tribeca co-op, a pricey divorce settlement, and probably a few "God-knows-what" charges sprinkled in for good measure. If there were a black hole in Manhattan that sucked up money, Dan had definitely found it.

But if $9 million had vanished, it also meant something else: there could still be up to $6 million left sitting in the Chase accounts back in New York. The Lebanon ops usually ran on about half a million in their combined local accounts, just enough for payroll, supplies, and the day-to-day grease to keep the machine moving.

The next morning, I hit the road for Lebanon. My job was to create two sets of financials—Dan's World and The Real World. Dan's version was the dreamscape: numbers massaged just right to calm Westinghouse Credit into thinking we were still worth the risk. My version was the cold truth. A survival roadmap for a company missing $9–15 million in cash and still expected to deliver on promises it never made.

While I was buried in spreadsheets and financial triage, Jim Murtha and Steve Trampe caught a flight to New York. They met with Dan and Alan Jacobs at Zellermayer Gratch & Jacobs, a slick law office on 57th and 3rd. That meeting was a five-minute farce.

Alan, a big guy with a loud voice, a fat cigar, flashy suspenders, and curly hair on retreat, told them that he couldn't advise the board anymore. Apparently, there was a conflict of interest. He was representing Dan personally now, which raised more than eyebrows. Alan had worked with Detroit Tool before, but Dan was the whale client with other juicy deals, so he jumped the fence. Loyalty didn't pay like Dan did.

Steve and Jim came back with nothing but a cab receipt. Total waste. I stayed in Lebanon the rest of the week, then returned to St. Louis for the weekend before boarding my go-to TWA Flight 468 to LaGuardia on Monday, October 22nd. By now, I could've done that trip blindfolded.

Once in New York, I handed Dan the cleaned-up financial projections for the Westinghouse proposal. Then I spent the rest of the week working on Trivest's new requests around their potential acquisition of The Shannon Group, an exhausting but oddly welcome distraction from the mess. But while I was knee-deep in the mess, Dan held a secret meeting, again. This time with Jim Murtha and Ken Goldberg somewhere off the radar in Manhattan. He showed them a single ledger sheet, listing around 25 separate cash transfers with dates and amounts—roughly $9 million in undocumented advances, but he refused to give them a copy. Just a peek.

Then came Halloween. Dan and I sat down with Dave Wessell at 1 Madison Avenue—an office that, ironically, looked more like a haunted house that day. Dan laid it all out for Dave; there was no more hiding. However, Dave, loyal as he was to the company, wasn't having it. He'd been in the trenches for over 25 years, building operations around the country. But finance wasn't his world. And now that world was cracking underneath him, and he didn't trust it, or Dan. And he said so.

We made the same ask again—return the money, or commit to a plan. Dan gave us the same answer: No.

The next morning, I handed Dan yet another clean, detailed Term Sheet—another lifeline, if we're being honest. It laid out a clear path to fixing the Problem. My proposal was simple: use the proceeds from The Shannon Group closing to pay back a hefty portion of the missing $9 million, with $5 million immediately. The rest was covered by a promissory note, $1 million a month until the full amount was paid back. It was clean, fair, and the last shot before we all went over the cliff together.

Dan gave me that signature half-smile and said, "Let's talk tomorrow."

Tomorrow came, and he punted again. "Let's talk Monday."

By Monday morning, November 5th, I was back in New York. I met Dan in his office, already knowing this wasn't going to end well. His new "repayment plan" was a joke—loose on structure, vague on timing, and flat-out insulting in scale. I immediately called the other board members. We all agreed: not acceptable.

And just like that, the walls finally came down.

That same afternoon, Dan called me back into his office. He leaned back in his chair, looked me in the eye, and delivered the line like a mafia boss: "You've become the best deal guy I've ever had, but I have to let you go. Your loyalty to the firm is in question."

That was it; no drama or speeches. It was just a quiet and surreal moment, the first time in my life I'd ever been fired. I packed my stuff, and no one said a word. No pats on the back and no goodbyes. I was radioactive at that point—persona non grata in a place I had once helped build from the ground up. The only person who acknowledged me was Matt Barry, an analyst from St. Louis. He knew who I was and that I wasn't the problem.

I left the office, walked to the apartment, grabbed my bags, and disappeared. At LaGuardia, I managed to grab a flight home to St. Louis. From the terminal payphone, I called my wife.

"Hey, can you pick me up from the airport?"

"What? You're coming home?"

"Yeah," I said. "Let's just say there's a hot deal brewing in the Midwest."

In the car on the way home from the airport, I told her as much as I could. She'd already sensed something was off – spouses always know. But what really shook her wasn't the story; it was seeing me there on a weekday, bags in hand, without a single travel plan or return ticket. And honestly? It shook me to my core, too.

The Dan era was over; the chase, the jet-setting, the multi-million-dollar fires. I was done. For the first time in years, I had nowhere to be, no deal to close, and no chaos to put out. It was an uneventful drive home, just Lynn, and a long road ahead. Whatever came next, it was going to start in St. Louis.

Chapter Eleven: Moving on Along

Tuesday, November 6th, was a day like no other. It was the ignition switch – my official departure from Kenmare was barely 24 hours old, but I'd already gone from cut loose to charging full-speed toward resolution. The Problem wasn't going to fix itself, and the longer it sat, the more it would fester.

First stop that morning: a meeting with Steve Trampe and the Midland Group guys. The second I stepped inside, the elephant in the room practically introduced itself. I was still a "Kenmare guy" in their eyes, and while Steve had vouched for me privately, trust doesn't transfer on a handshake. Still, they listened, and they gave me something better than trust: autonomy. I had the green light to do what

I thought made sense, so that I could fix it, and do it quietly and quickly.

They suggested a lawyer, Joe Lehrer, partner at Greensfelder Hemker & Gale in downtown St. Louis. The name was familiar, and not in a bad way. They said he was smart, fast, and tough, which was exactly what I needed. But before any legal moves, I needed to check in with someone who actually ran the day-to-day. I drove to Lebanon, Missouri, for an early morning meeting on Wednesday, November 7th, with Dave Wessell. I told him everything: my firing, the mess Dan left behind, and my plan to work with Midland to make things right. Dave didn't need a long speech; he'd given Dan years of loyalty, but his heart was with Detroit Tool. He was in.

We didn't waste a second. That same morning, Dave and I walked into Commerce Bank like a pair of outlaws ready to reclaim stolen territory. We opened a whole new slate of accounts—mirror images of the originals—but with one crucial change: Dan and Andy were locked out. No signature authority or access. The company's day-to-day money was back in safe hands.

I returned to St. Louis with momentum and met with Joe Lehrer at his office. In ten minutes, I knew we had the right guy. Joe was sharp, no-nonsense, and fired up. I laid out everything for him: the Westinghouse loan documents, shareholder agreements, and our previous term sheets to Dan. Joe's feedback was fast and focused. He had the kind of mind that could smell trouble before it walked in the door. Then, from Joe's office, I called Dave Shockey at Westinghouse Credit. I told him, point-blank, the October 10th meeting with Dan was a total con job. We needed a private sit-down, just us, with no Kenmare and no distractions. He agreed.

Then I rang Wessell again and told him to prep the Detroit Tool plane that would lift us out on the evening of Thursday, November 8th, straight to Pittsburgh. A covert run, just the way we needed it. And while I was tying up loose ends, I checked in with my old contacts at Bowles Hollowell Conner & Co. The Shannon Group deal was still solid, but they'd been blindsided by the news of my exit. "Stunned" was the word. I promised them the real story when the time was right.

The chessboard had changed. Now it was our move.

By Thursday morning, I was back in Joe Lehrer's office, going over more details about how the Problem started and everything that led up to it. We went through every detail—names, dates, docs, motives—tightening the timeline and making an air-tight strategy. This wasn't about revenge anymore; this was about precision. Joe needed to know why each document mattered, what each piece of evidence meant, and how all the pieces fit. I was like building a missile.

Then I made the call to Dave Shockey. We set a private meeting at Westinghouse Credit's downtown Pittsburgh office for Friday morning. By 5:00 p.m. Thursday, Detroit Tool's plane—our trusty Rockwell 690B Turbo Commander—had landed at Spirit Airport, wheels still warm from its run out of Lebanon. Joe, Jim Murtha, and I jumped in. No limo, no fanfare. We just took off into the evening sky. Our destination was Pittsburgh, and our business now was survival.

That Friday, November 9th, we walked into Westinghouse Credit with our backs straight and stories straight. I gave Shockey the full rundown and told him about the internal coup and how we had taken back the controls, cut Kenmare's access to the bank accounts, and isolated the cancer before it could spread. Then I showed him the "real world" projections I had run—clean and sober with no fluff. It was going to be tight, but Detroit Tool could make it, even without the $15 million in limbo. All we needed was a little breathing room and some faith.

To his credit, Shockey didn't flinch. He listened carefully, nodded in the right places, and asked the right questions. He didn't make promises, but he made space. He said they'd consider continued support, but warned that a

Default Notice would hit us the following week. Not great, but not terrible either. But for now, we had a little more time to build something stronger.

The real heavy lifting started the next day. I parked myself at the Greensfelder law firm's office like a squatter with a purpose. Joe and I burned through the weekend, drafting yet another Term Sheet—our oldest, most dialed-in proposal yet. But that wasn't all: we built an affidavit too, a grenade of truth wrapped in legal jargon. This was no soft memo. This was a blow-by-blow of everything Dan had done, everything we had discovered, and everything we were ready to expose. The goal was to obtain a Temporary Restraining Order to freeze Dan in his tracks, especially from unloading or laundering his shares in The Shannon Group before we could make things right.

Joe brought in backup, a seasoned attorney from New York he'd worked with before. Between the three of us, the affidavit became a scalpel and a spotlight. I wasn't just a witness, I was the inside man. And then, I still had about five grand in airline ticket credits tucked away in my briefcase, already paid for by Kenmare. Some people stash snacks, but I carried surprise mobility. That Monday morning, I used it for one last mission. The hunt wasn't over; the game had just changed.

Just like I used to when I wore the Kenmare badge, I put on my most classy suit—crisp white shirt, a navy tie, and polished black shoes—and caught the Monday morning flight, TWA 468, bound for LaGuardia. It was November 12th, and I wasn't flying in for a board meeting or a pitch this time. This was a retrieval operation; a surgical mission, if you may.

The cab dropped me off at 1 Madison Avenue, same as always. But today, I wasn't heading left to the security desk that protected the elevator banks to the upper floors, including the floor where we used to make deals and write checks that made careers—or destroyed them. No, this time I walked straight through the brass-finished double doors of the Chase branch tucked away on the first floor.

There was something poetic about it; I was using the same tools they once handed me—the very accounts they opened under the banner of progress—to pull the rug out from under them. Inside the bank, I waited patiently, holding a sleek black folder that held every routing and account number I needed. After a few minutes, a young but clearly seasoned account officer ushered me to her desk in the center of the lobby. She smiled professionally.

"How can I help you today?"

I gave her my name, handed over two forms of ID, and explained calmly but firmly that we needed to move funds between accounts. These were accounts I had helped establish in the first place—back when Dan and Andy still trusted me and back when I was their guy. But they hadn't gotten around to changing the signatories yet. That was their first mistake.

"Let's begin," I said.

"Please transfer the entire balance from the Detroit Tool and Engineering Company account number 10203040 into its new twin at Commerce Bank in Lebanon, Missouri. Routing number 101000019, account 40302010."

She typed, clicked, and scanned the screen. "That balance is $370-something thousand dollars, sir."

"Good. Let's keep going."

Next came Detroit Tool Metal Products. "From 10207080 at Chase to 40306050 at Commerce. Same routing."

"Balance: about $180,000."

"Perfect. Now let's finish it."

The last transfer was from the holding company—Detroit Tool Group, Inc. "From account 10201112 to 40301109 at Commerce."

"That's $420,000 and change."

Less than a million bucks. That was the haul. I sat there, staring at the final total, and my heart sank. All that effort—the early flights, the chess-like moves, the planning, the cab rides across the city—and for what? A payout that didn't even crack seven figures. Crap. Dan must've drained another $4 million somewhere. Just gone, and vanished into thin air.

I sat in stunned silence, disappointment tightening in my chest. What had he done with that kind of money? Where had it gone? This wasn't sloppy accounting; this was a full-blown, grade-A mess. I started gathering my papers, nodded politely, and was halfway out of my seat when the account officer, almost offhandedly, asked a question that stopped me cold.

"And how about Detroit Tool Group, Inc.—account number 10201516?"

I froze in place, my fingers still resting on the edge of the chair, and my eyes dropped immediately back to the carefully crafted list I put together. That account—Detroit Tool Group, Inc., number 10201516— was completely unfamiliar to me. I did not initiate the opening of that account when I opened the other 3 Chase accounts. It was a total wildcard. The account materialized completely out of nowhere.

And yet, here it was, suddenly rising to the surface, called out in real time by the account officer like a ghost manifesting out of the shadows and asking to be seen. It caught me completely off guard, but instinct and training kicked in. I masked the surprise that surged through my chest, keeping my expression flat, my voice steady. Years of negotiation, late-night strategy sessions, and maybe even a little leftover showmanship from high school drama class—thank you, Mr. Hicks—held me together in that moment.

"Yes," I said, calmly and without hesitation, "Please transfer to Detroit Tool Group, Inc. Commerce Bank account number 40301109, routing number 101000019."

She didn't flinch, didn't blink—just glanced at her monitor and read the number back to me with the same detached tone she'd used for the others.

"Yes, sir," she said, "That account currently holds just over $4 million."

And just like that, everything changed.

It felt like a silent firework exploded behind my eyes. I nodded politely, thanked her as if it was just another Monday errand, and walked calmly out of the Chase branch. A few blocks later, I hailed a cab to LaGuardia and finally let myself breathe.

Dan and Andy had stashed away a secret war chest—one they assumed was out of reach. And yet, thanks to one small administrative oversight by an unaware bank officer, it now belonged to us. The underdog had just pulled off the heist of the season.

I caught the next flight back to St. Louis with a grin slapped across my face and $5 million back under Detroit Tool's local control. That wasn't just money, it was leverage. It was bargaining power. It was a signal to everyone watching that we were not dead in the water. When I shared the news with Dave Wessell, Steve Trampe, the Midland guys, and Dave Shockey, their reactions were electric. Even Shockey, who reminded me that the Default Notice was still coming, couldn't hide his shock.

That night, I got a call at home from Andy Mayer.

"I just had to call and say... you're *good*," he said, half admiring, half defeated.

I thanked him and told him good luck. Because deep down, I didn't blame Andy. He was young, loyal, and maybe a little naive. He was following orders, but real trouble was still sitting at the top. And while $5 million was a huge win, it was only one battle, and the war was far from over. We still had a $10 million hole and a majority shareholder standing in the way.

Chapter Twelve: Taking Off the Gloves

Dan was absolutely incensed when Andy told him I had moved $5 million right from under their noses, almost literally, with the Chase bank located just 20 floors under the Kenmare office. He was so mad, he apparently vowed that he would never want to see me or talk to me again. That didn't stop him from maintaining a cordial relationship with Steve Trampe, of course. Dan always had his strategic alliances, even when betrayed. But the blow I delivered by being able to move that cash, in the manner and with the speed I did, was a devastating one. It wasn't just the money, it was the message: we're watching, we're acting, and we're not going to let this spiral any further, not without consequences.

That weekend, we amended the affidavit to reflect the $5 million that had been successfully retrieved and transferred back to the newly established Commerce Bank accounts in Lebanon. We wasted no time — a notarized copy of the updated affidavit was overnighted to the attorneys' office in New York on Tuesday, November 13th. The sense of urgency wasn't just practical — it was existential. Westinghouse Credit had already declared the plaintiffs in default. Every minute mattered.

By some divine alignment or perhaps just a moment of judicial clarity, the judge with the Supreme Court of the State of New York, County of New York, reviewed our filing and granted the Temporary Restraining Order the very same day. That was no small feat. The TRO, once served, would effectively freeze Dan and Kenmare in their tracks, barring them from transferring, dissipating, or otherwise manipulating any property in which they had an interest. It was a decisive maneuver — the legal equivalent of putting the king in check. But the board was still crowded, and the next moves, starting with serving Dan, had to be just as calculated.

The affidavit itself, sworn and signed under penalty of perjury, laid out every stone of the crooked path Dan had engineered — a meticulous roadmap of fiduciary betrayal, internal obstruction, and financial sleight-of-hand. Line by line, it exposed how he leveraged his authority, concealed information, and stonewalled board members. It detailed the various meetings, evasive responses, and cryptic ledgers — all of which painted a picture of a man who had taken control of a company's finances and turned them into his personal war chest.

What stunned many, myself included, was how long he had kept the operation running. Dan, operating under the thin veil of strategic investment, had siphoned nearly $9 million through roughly 25 separate "advances," which he claimed had all been invested "on behalf of the plaintiffs." The problem was that there was no paper trail or accountability; just oral reassurances and the elusive promise of undocumented notes. And then, conveniently, Kenmare, the supposed obligor on those advances, just happened to have no means of repaying them.

The affidavit also called out, point-blank, how Dan refused to allow outside counsel to advise the board on the matter, citing a conflict of interest with their current firm — a firm, mind you, that had been representing Dan himself all along. In hindsight, it was an orchestrated effort to keep everyone in the dark. And it worked, until it didn't.

There was a line in the affidavit that resonated louder than the others, not because of its legal weight, but because of its raw, unvarnished truth: *"Despite repeated requests by members of the Boards of Directors... Dan has refused to disclose the whereabouts of the advances he received or to return the funds."*

It was simple, yet damning.

This wasn't just about misappropriation; this was about a betrayal of trust, of governance, of every fiduciary principle underpinning corporate responsibility. And for me, personally, it was confirmation that I had been right to act when I did, to fight tooth and nail to regain control, and to ensure that at least some of that money, that oxygen, was returned to the system before it collapsed entirely.

The affidavit was now a matter of public record. Dan could rage all he wanted, but the machine had been set in motion. What followed would be a series of hearings, depositions, audits, and more late nights in law offices than I care to remember. But on that day, November 13th, 1990, the tide had turned.

And whether he liked it or not, Dan was going to have to watch it all play out from the sidelines.

With the Temporary Restraining Order granted, the next step, serving Dan, was going to be tricky. If we could get that done, maybe we could finally start moving the ball forward. The Problem — capital "P," now really *emphasized* at this point — was suffocating every attempt at negotiation.

Dan was unpredictable and increasingly hostile, and the TRO was, hopefully, the leverage we needed to snap him out of his power spiral and bring him back to the table.

But here was the real issue: serving Dan was going to be hell. Not because he was dodging us, but because getting close enough to even *try* was a logistical nightmare. The Kenmare office was located at 1 Madison Avenue, which just happened to be the world headquarters for Metropolitan Life Insurance Company. That building wasn't just secure, it was practically a fortress.

There was a well-oiled security operation running the front desks. Every single person entering the upper floors of the building needed a photo ID security badge just to get past the first line of defense. Want to reach the tower where the Kenmare offices were? That required presenting a valid Metropolitan Life building ID or getting a live confirmation phone call from someone inside. No Metropolitan Life building ID or live confirmation call, no entry. Full stop. Elevators wouldn't even move without it. The process server didn't stand a chance.

To make matters worse, the building had multiple points of entry, including access from underground subway stops on the #6 and #4 lines. That meant Dan could move in and out from various directions, often bypassing the main 1 Madison Avenue entrance entirely. It was like trying to serve legal papers to a ghost in a vault. We weren't just trying to hand a manila envelope to a guy in a suit; we were trying to crack into one of the most secure buildings in Manhattan without a badge or backup.

The whole operation had to be covert, agile, and creatively aggressive.

At the time, I must have been one of the busiest unemployed 33-year-olds on the planet. I wasn't drawing a paycheck, but I was clocking in harder and longer than most CEOs. And the irony? Most of the drama, like the calls, the planning, and the coordination, was happening in Missouri, practically in my backyard. The eye of the storm was right here. From Missouri boardrooms, in St. Louis and at Detroit Tool in Lebanon, to New York City courtrooms, I was straddling two very different worlds, doing everything I could to bring clarity and control to the chaos.

Every so often, I'd allow myself a minute to wonder: *What comes after this?* The Problem was consuming my time, energy, and every last drop of adrenaline. I didn't have a roadmap beyond it. But I also wasn't panicking — St. Louis isn't exactly a hotbed for M&A professionals, and I knew the options would be limited if I chose to stay. Part of me toyed with the idea of returning to New York and getting back into the private equity world. But then there was my investment banking connection in Charlotte, North

Carolina — Bowles Hollowell Conner & Co. was looking more interesting by the day. I'd built solid relationships with several of their principals through the Pangborn and Shannon Group deals. There was mutual respect and momentum.

Still, I had the luxury of not needing to make that decision right away. I didn't have a huge personal burn rate. No massive mortgage, no expensive habits. I could breathe. And more importantly, I could think clearly — without panic, without emotion — which turned out to be one of the biggest advantages I had as we worked to resolve the rest of this mess.

That's when a more sobering realization started to sink in; this whole ordeal — the lawsuits, the filings, the financial gymnastics — wasn't really about running a business. It wasn't about the work or the products or the people who made them. It was about *paper*. One rectangular, landscape-oriented slip of ink and fiber: a stock certificate – that was the crown jewel, and that's what they were willing to burn it all down for.

Meanwhile, there were nearly 400 men and women working on shop floors and behind desks in Lebanon, Missouri, who had no idea what was happening behind the scenes. They were manufacturing, shipping, and hustling, all while the financial puppet masters bled the company dry with convertible notes, insider transfers, and forged alliances. These were families with mortgages, kids, dreams — all living in a town of 12,000 people, completely unaware that a few men in suits were playing a dangerous game that could cost them everything.

The contrast was staggering; one world dealt in power plays and signatures while the other dealt in sweat and production schedules. One lived in courtrooms and conference calls, while the other punched timecards and ran production machinery. And somewhere in the middle of that collision stood little old me, trying to keep the whole thing from going up in flames.

Getting the rest of the Problem resolved was going to be anything but simple. Dan made it clear: he wouldn't deal with me directly. No calls, meetings, or even a voicemail. Everything would go through Alan Jacobs, his attorney. And while that could've been a brick wall, it turned out to be a small advantage. Alan and I had a decent rapport. He wasn't the type to throw grenades for fun. And thankfully, Dan hadn't replaced him with a new firm yet, which meant Alan still had context, history, and at least some incentive to see this resolved quickly.

Joe Lehrer, the attorney with Greensfelder, and I decided not to make a fuss. We let it go. There was too much ground to cover to waste time on a game of legal musical chairs.

Besides, we had work to do. We had already started drafting a Term Sheet over the weekend and got it faxed to Alan on November 14th. The document was meant to be a framework, something tangible to anchor the discussion. We didn't expect Dan to agree to every clause, but we needed to get him to the table. And now, with the TRO granted and the affidavit on file, we had potential leverage. *Real* potential leverage. The hunt to serve Dan wasn't over, but the game had an excellent chance of really changing in our favor.

The Term Sheet we sent over wasn't just a set of legal proposals; it was a full-scale financial intervention. A grown-up timeout with teeth. After weeks of being dragged through the muck, we needed a hard reset, and this was it. The goal wasn't to cut Dan completely out, just not yet. The strategy was smarter than that. This proposal would give him the dignity of remaining a shareholder in Detroit Tool Group but without the reins. No control over the bank accounts. No access to the operational dials and levers. He could stay on the ship; he just wouldn't be allowed to steer it into another iceberg.

This was the olive branch, with a steel core. The deal we outlined struck a balance. It allowed Dan to keep about half of what I estimated he'd eventually pocket from the sale of The Shannon Group, provided he stopped the bleeding and came clean, now. In the long run, the Term Sheet also laid out the path for a clean break: an eventual sale of Detroit Tool Group that would give all stakeholders, including Westinghouse Credit Corp., a chance to walk away whole. But the message was crystal clear — the days of freelancing with company money were over.

Term Sheet Highlights

- **Full Disclosure, In Writing:** First and foremost, Dan had to come clean. Every single cash transfer he'd authorized had to be detailed, signed, and sent over — then verified by Andy Mayer. No more secrets or side channels.

- **$10+ Million Payback Plan:** Dan and Kenmare Capital Corp. would sign a binding promissory note for the total amount of all those unauthorized transfers, plus interest. The repayment schedule was aggressive: $2.5 million due on November 21st — the expected closing date for The Shannon Group sale — followed by $1 million per month until the full balance was paid.

- **Collateral, Collateral, Collateral:** The note wasn't going to float on good intentions. It would be backed fully by all of Dan's Detroit Tool Group shares, which I estimated to be worth $7.5 million (after knocking off a $500,000 loan he had with Southside National Bank). On top of that, his shares in The Shannon Group, worth about $4.1 million net of a $900,000 IRS lien, were on the table. And, if that wasn't enough, all of his shares in another Kenmare Capital portfolio company, Family Bargain Stores Holdings, Inc. (valued at $1.2 million by Montgomery Securities), were also pledged until the outstanding note balance dropped below $5 million.

- **Management Fees Redirected:** Any management fees owed to Kenmare Capital would now be redirected toward repaying the note. No more passive income streams while we cleaned up his mess.
- **Control Shift:** The strategic and operational direction of Detroit Tool would now sit with the majority of the board of directors, not Dan. Period.
- **Cash Consolidation:** Any remaining funds in Detroit Tool's New York accounts would be immediately transferred to Commerce Bank in Lebanon, Missouri. Dan and Andy Mayer's days of moving money around like chess pieces were done. All cash management operations would now run through Lebanon. Andy would give up all signatory authority.

- **Governance Overhaul:** We proposed amending Detroit Tool Group's Articles of Incorporation and Bylaws to allow any two board members to call a board meeting. It was a small change, but a powerful one. No more stalling or hiding behind procedural red tape.

- **Borrowing Freeze:** No more drawing down Detroit Tool's Westinghouse Credit Corp. line. That well was closed. Full disclosure would also be made to Westinghouse the moment the Term Sheet was executed. They deserved to know what kind of circus their money had wandered into.

- **Default Protocols:** If Dan defaulted on the note, his Detroit Tool Group shares would be retired and converted into treasury stock. An independent valuation would be conducted. If the shares turned out to be worth more than the balance owed, Detroit Tool Group would pay him the difference — but if they came up short, he'd owe Detroit Tool Group. Either way, five annual payments would settle the dust.

- **Legal Firewalls:** To keep this clean, Dan's legal counsel going forward would have to be completely independent — someone with no prior ties to Detroit Tool. No conflicts. No backdoors.

Let's be honest: this wasn't just a document, it was a leash and a countdown clock, all rolled into one. It held Dan accountable in ways he couldn't dodge or dilute. And it gave the rest of us a real shot at unwinding the damage without triggering a full corporate collapse.

Of course, we didn't yet know the exact amount Dan had moved around. That part was still under audit, but even without the final figure, the Term Sheet structured repayment and collateralization well north of the estimated $10 million balance still in question. By my calculations, we were looking at $12.8 million in total coverage: $7.5 million in Detroit Tool Group equity, $4.1 million from The Shannon Group, and $1.2 million from Family Bargain Stores. It wasn't just enough, it was smart.

And as I read the proposal back to myself, a smile crept across my face. This wasn't the work of an angry investor or a desperate partner; this was the return of the commercial banker in me — sleeves rolled, pencils sharp, rules reasserted. There was no adrenaline in it. Just discipline, precision, and a structure tight enough to hold water in a wind tunnel and fair enough to avoid courtroom theatrics.

It was time to see if Dan was ready to deal with reality. Just when I thought we might be inching toward a real solution, a fax came in through the machine at the Greensfelder law office on November 15th. The sender?

Kenmare Capital Corp. The document? A new proposal from Dan — this time dressed up as a "restructuring" of the promissory note we had put on the table the day before.

At first glance, it looked like an attempt to meet us halfway. On closer inspection, it was anything but.

Here's what Dan's revised plan proposed:

- **Disclosure... again:** Dan would supposedly make a full written disclosure of all cash transfers, which would then be verified by Andy Mayer. This, of course, was the same condition we had already demanded in our original Term Sheet — and by now, felt more like a formality than a gesture of goodwill.
- **Watered-down repayment**: Rather than the $2.5 million up front followed by $1 million monthly, Dan's version pushed the first payment back to December 1st with $1 million monthly thereafter — no upfront lump sum, no pressure.
- **Weakened collateral:** The note would be backed by shares of another Kenmare Capital portfolio company, Old American Stores (which he valued at $3.75 million — a number we hadn't vetted), and just one-third of his shares in Family Bargain Stores, which he pegged at $400,000. For reference, our plan had locked in all of his Detroit Tool Group, Shannon

Group, and Family Bargain Stores shares, with coverage north of $12 million. This new package barely cleared $4 million and was based entirely on his numbers.

- **Board handcuffs:** Any payment or expenditure by Dan, other than his salary, management fees to Kenmare, or "ordinary business expenses," would need approval from a majority of the board. Sounds good on paper, right? Except in Dan's world, $50,000–$60,000 in monthly American Express charges qualified as "ordinary business." He was trying to bake in the same toxic spending that got us here in the first place.

- **Independent counsel... again:** Dan would agree to be represented by independent legal counsel, with no prior ties to Detroit Tool. A familiar clause, and one we had already written.

In short, this proposal was a watered-down echo of our own, with all the strings loosened or clipped entirely. The whole structure was built around protecting Dan's freedom to keep moving, not resolving the Problem. He had cut out the most important collateral, his soon-to-be-liquid Shannon Group shares, and kept the bulk of his Family Bargain Stores equity off the table. These were the two hottest assets in his portfolio, and he was trying to lock them away while tossing us scraps. It was classic Dan: nod in agreement with one hand while rearranging the deck with the other.

We weren't surprised in the least. The Term Sheet Joe and I had sent to Alan just a day before was serious and air-tight. It put hard numbers on the table, pulled the plug on Dan's access to cash, and created real legal leverage. If adopted, it could have ended the games and brought real closure to a mess that was threatening to pull down more than just Dan. But Dan wasn't interested in real closure, not if it meant losing control of Detroit Tool — or giving up the windfall he was sitting on from The Shannon Group deal. So instead, he tried to buy time. The proposal that came through the fax was a smokescreen, dressed up as a compromise.

And it almost worked. The Midland Group guys, our minority partners in this drama, initially showed some interest in taking Dan's offer seriously. They saw a document that, on its face, looked like a step in the right direction. A quick resolution, a clear plan; a way to end the headache without triggering World War III. But then we walked them through the fine print. We pointed out the landmines hidden in plain sight:

- There was still no transfer of control over Detroit Tool's business operations or cash.

- The collateral offered was thin, illiquid, and self-appraised.
- Dan still considered tens of thousands of dollars in personal charges to be "ordinary business expenses."
- Westinghouse Credit Corp., our lender and a crucial player, would almost certainly balk at this structure. If they walked, the whole house of cards would go down.
- And perhaps most important: Dan wasn't going to repay the funds unless forced to. Full stop.

Once they saw it clearly, the Midland Group guys backed off fast.

In the end, Dan's proposal was exactly what we suspected it would be: a stalling tactic. A ploy. A shiny object meant to distract just long enough for The Shannon Group deal to close — and for him to collect the cash. He was running out the clock, plain and simple.

Dan knew emotions were running high and that people were anxious. Some were scared of losing their investment altogether. And so, he played it just right, not by fighting back, but by dangling *just enough* hope to slow things down. His strategy wasn't to defuse the bomb. It was to wait until the wires were buried under so much paperwork that no one could remember which one to cut.

It was now obvious: Dan had no intention of solving *the Problem* on fair terms. His proposal wasn't a bridge; it was a decoy. The war chest he'd once held at Chase was going to be rebuilt, and the Shannon Group sale was the key. Whether he was preparing for a fight or gearing up for a leveraged buyout with someone like Midland, one thing was clear: He was playing chess. The rest of us had to decide whether to keep reacting or make a move of our own. Getting Dan served was an absolute must.

Chapter Thirteen: Another Hit

Dan wasn't one to let all his efforts keel over and die. Not without a fight, anyway. If anything, he was doubling down. After we delivered a sharp and unapologetic rejection of the November 15th proposal, he pivoted yet again, dropping another manipulative idea into the lap of the Midland Group: "Why don't you just buy me out of Detroit Tool?"

It was classic Dan; just when things were tightening around him, he feigned surrender and offered an exit ramp that looked too good to ignore. And for a fleeting moment, it worked. The Midland Group guys—good men, serious investors, and still hopeful that this mess could be solved without a courtroom—perked up. Dan had dangled yet another lifeline, and they reached toward it, thinking maybe, just maybe, this would be the resolution they'd been grinding toward for several weeks.

But to me, it was obvious that this was another stalling maneuver. Another hit in Dan's psychological war game. The supposed buyout idea was smoke, not fire. There were no terms. No math, no timing, and nothing that smelled like real business. This wasn't a deal; it was another delay, and another way to inch closer to the closing of The Shannon Group deal. Dan was bleeding time from us and squeezing opportunity from every ticking second. A lawyer by training, he knew exactly what he was doing. And he was absolutely *not* negotiating in good faith. The phrase they use in the legal world – "*bad faith bargaining*"- *m*ight as well have now been written on his letterhead.

I couldn't speak openly with my contacts at Bowles Hollowell Conner & Co. about the specifics of The Shannon Group deal, but I did manage to make a call. Carefully sidestepping anything confidential, I got the information I needed: the new closing date for The Shannon Group was officially moved up to November 20th. One day earlier than last reported, which didn't help our already-crunched timeline. But five days were five days, and we had to move fast.

Time was short, and the usual methods of serving Dan with the Temporary Restraining Order were failing. We had tried a handful of traditional approaches, but Dan—cagey, paranoid, and now likely anticipating legal retaliation—was staying slippery. Serving him without a trap wasn't going to work. We needed a setup, a play, or at the very least, something he wouldn't see coming.

We knew Dan's psychological map. He believed that Jim Murtha and Lee Wielansky were tightly wired into all the key negotiations. He knew they were serious players. He also assumed Ken Goldberg, the advisory director with a financial stake, but no operational control, might be a softer target. Maybe even a sympathetic ear.

That assumption? It became our angle.

Ken wasn't involved in Midland Group's day-to-day real estate business. He had his own shop, his own developments. But he *was* a member of the Midland Detroit Tool investment entity. He had skin in the game, even if his hands weren't in the dirt. And most importantly, he had credibility with Dan. If anyone could draw Dan out from his foxhole and get him to lower his guard, it was Ken.

We laid it out for him. The clock was ticking, and Dan was heading to Atlanta soon to close the Shannon Group deal. We needed to catch him before that happened, and we needed someone he wouldn't see coming. Ken was that someone. To his credit, Ken didn't blink. He agreed to suit up and step into the arena, not just for his investment, but for the group. For the principal. For the idea that games like this can't be allowed to win. What came next would be fast, precise, and, if we played it right, a checkmate move before Dan ever saw it coming.

Ken Goldberg was the kind of guy who could walk into any room, flash a perfectly timed smile, and make people believe he was there to help, not cause a world of hurt. So, when it came time to deliver a surprise that needed just the right mix of charm, discretion, and precision, Ken was our man.

He called Dan the way only Ken could: smooth, unthreatening, and casually persuasive. He told him he'd flown into New York for a bit of shopping, something about catching the new holiday displays on Fifth Avenue, and was staying at The Plaza Hotel. He suggested they meet for breakfast at 9:00 a.m. the next morning, Friday, November 16th. The pitch was simple: *Let's talk about how I might help bridge the gap between you and the Midland guys.* Dan, who saw Ken as harmless, maybe even useful, agreed without hesitation.

Ken packed a bag that afternoon, jumped on a flight to LaGuardia, and checked into The Plaza. We promised him that if the plan worked, he'd earn his stay, his own little encore for the earlier "Chase Manhattan Surprise." This was a game of chess, and Ken was about to checkmate a king. The next morning, at 7:30 sharp, Ken met the process server downstairs in the hotel lobby. Timing was everything. Ken needed eyes on Dan's entourage; if he brought anyone along, we needed to know, but the meeting went just as we'd hoped. Dan, unusually punctual, showed up solo, clean-shaven, donning a dark suit, and with the same old confidence. He walked into the gilded dining room expecting croissants and negotiation. Instead, he got served.

Just as he settled into his chair, the process server appeared behind him like a ghost from Wall Street's past. "Mr. Dan Sullivan?" he asked. "Yes," Dan replied, caught completely off guard. Then, without so much as flinching, the server handed over the Temporary Restraining Order. According to Ken, the look on Dan's face was nothing short of priceless.

And Ken was cool as ever. He didn't touch the menu, hadn't ordered so much as a coffee. As we reminded him that morning, no food means no delay. He stood up, gave Dan a polite nod, and exited the dining room with the calm of a man who had just landed the perfect uppercut without getting a wrinkle in his suit. *Mission accomplished*. Another win on New York City soil.

With just four days left before the closing of The Shannon Group deal, the TRO delivery was a clutch move.

It sent a clear legal warning and hit hard, emotionally. But as we regrouped and celebrated this mini-victory, one question kept circling overhead like a hawk: Would this finally be enough to drag Dan into the daylight, to get him to negotiate in *actual* good faith?

As for Ken, the man deserved his flowers. Always manicured to the minute, his tan perpetually perfect, and his slicked-back jet-black hair looking like it had been combed by the angels themselves, he was the epitome of polish. In his mid-forties, Ken was exactly the right guy to pull off a story about luxury shopping and a stay at The Plaza. And Dan? He bought the whole thing.

The truth was, Ken had always kept one foot outside the blast radius. Though a partner in the Detroit Tool Group investment vehicle, he'd smartly chosen observer status—not a full director, no legal exposure. He could attend the meetings, share his views, but when the bullets flew, he had plausible deniability and legal insulation. And now, ironically, it was that outsider status that made him the perfect insider to land this strike. We were proud of him. No question. In fact, this might have been the most heroic thing Ken had ever done in his professional life. And when the dust eventually settled, it turned out he'd been right all along—observer, not operator, was the safest seat in the house.

Despite the tactical win at The Plaza, I found myself in an odd limbo. The thrill of the moment had passed, the adrenaline had cooled, and reality set in. I had no formal role, no title, and no office to return to. I was a free agent with nowhere to report; a man between missions. The truth is, for all my knowledge of Dan's financial web, for all the finesse I'd developed in M&A and the capital markets, I was now floating, useful, but unanchored. It was as if I'd stepped off a moving train and the platform hadn't been built yet. Thankfully, the week didn't end that way.

Jim Murtha of Midland Group called that Friday evening, his tone calm and confident, and he came across as someone who meant what he said. He invited me out for drinks at the restaurant in his office complex, the kind of place where the booths are too big and the lights are too low, designed for quiet deals and confident whispers. We talked about the wild week, about what we'd pulled off, and about how much more there was to do. He didn't sugarcoat it. Dan might've been cornered, but the beast still had fight left in him. Detroit Tool was a mess, and unwinding his grip would take precision and persistence.

Then, as casually as someone might offer you a seat at their poker game, Jim asked if I wanted to work out of their office starting Monday morning. November 19th. Just like that, I was back in the game. Jim always was one of those guys who didn't need to boast, and the kind who didn't need to raise his voice to make a point. In his early forties, real estate in his DNA, he carried himself like someone who knew where the bodies were buried but never needed to dig them up. He had that blend of Midwestern charm and street smarts you rarely find in the boardroom. His silver hair was cropped close, and the slight belly under his sports coat told you he was comfortable in his skin.

His girlfriend, Lisa, was in her twenties; tall, polished, and cool under pressure. Her job at Greensfelder, Hemker & Gale gave her a front-row seat to high-stakes legal drama, and she knew who was good and who was just making a splash for the sake of it. It was Lisa who pointed us toward Joe Lehrer, the attorney who would later prove to be one of the key players in handling the Detroit Tool mess.

Jim's partner, Lee Wielansky, shared an oversized office with him at Midland. The two of them had the kind of friendship you could build a business on. When I arrived on Monday, Jim walked me around the office like I was a new hire at a startup company, introducing me to ten or twelve staffers as "someone helping us with a very special investment." Translation: *"He's on the team, but don't ask questions."*

My new "office" was...cozy. No windows, probably once a storage closet, but it had a desk, a chair, a phone, and a working computer. After about a week of operating out of my house, lawyer's offices, and side tables, it felt like a command center. It was exactly what I needed at the time: quiet, contained, and just under the radar. I didn't care about the square footage. What mattered was that the mission still had momentum, and now, I had a base. The next phase was coming, and we were going to need every bit of space, brainpower, and backchannel to finish what we'd started.

Had the closing of The Shannon Group gone through before Dan was served with the TRO, we would have been looking at a perfect storm. Not just a drawn-out, bruising legal slugfest—but a potentially fatal blow to Detroit Tool itself. Westinghouse Credit Corp., already watching from the sidelines with a nervous finger on the kill switch, might've taken that as the final sign to pull the plug on the credit lines. If they had, the company would've been dead in the water—liquidity gone, operations frozen, and trust shattered. The entire Detroit Tool structure was teetering, and this one move—the timing of the TRO—was a critical pin holding the whole thing together.

Dan, at this point, was 0 and 2 in terms of battles in the ongoing war. First, the Chase Manhattan maneuver caught him flat-footed. Then, the Plaza Hotel breakfast turned into an ambush, since he never saw it coming. Being served with a Temporary Restraining Order just as he sat down for breakfast at the Plaza Hotel was the kind of sucker punch that throws off your sense of control. For someone like Dan, who prided himself on being top dog, this had to be a devastating check to the chin.

But it wasn't just Dan who was blindsided. The law firm of Zellermayer, Gratch, and Jacobs—his legal lifeline—was likely just as perplexed. Dan had been a golden goose to them for years. Endless legal wranglings, transactions, disputes—he was a steady stream of billable hours. Alan, his lead attorney, had been walking a tightrope for several weeks. We had already waived any conflict concerns to keep things moving, but Alan's continued involvement was starting to look more like a gamble than a legal strategy. He was risking not only his firm's reputation, but possibly his own.

You can almost picture the scene in their offices: phones ringing off the hook, tense voices behind closed doors, junior partners being told to clear their calendars. Alan probably spent that Friday lighting up every line in his Rolodex, sending shockwaves through the Shannon Group deal team. The closing had been scheduled for Tuesday, in Atlanta. Everyone was expecting champagne and signatures. Instead, Alan had to deliver the news that Dan had "hit a snag", a gentle way of saying he'd been legally neutered.

The TRO stripped Dan of his ability to transfer his shares; that was the dagger. Without control of his equity, the entire transaction hit a wall. No matter how far along the paperwork was, no matter how many lawyers and bankers were circling the conference table in Atlanta, it wasn't happening; not on Tuesday, and certainly not with Dan boxed in.

It was a power move, and one that changed the energy in the room. Momentum was ours. Now it was Dan and his lawyers who had to recalibrate, rethink, and scramble. And while we knew this wasn't the end of the war, for the first time, it felt like we had the upper hand.

When word of "a snag" started to leak, the guys over at Bowles Hollowell Conner & Co., the investment bankers handling The Shannon Group sale, were among the first to smell blood, and they knew exactly where to look for the fire. They'd been watching the deal unfold like a Wall Street thriller, and my sudden exit from Kenmare was a plot twist they hadn't seen coming. In their world, timing is everything, and coincidences are rarely innocent. The connection between my abrupt departure and the delay in closing the Shannon Group transaction was too tight to ignore.

I imagine their first call wasn't to Trivest or any of the players on the buyer's side. It was to me. By Friday afternoon, the phone rang. Not even 48 hours had passed since I had reached out to them, trying to sniff out details on the revised closing date. And now, they were calling me, fishing for clarity without ever asking for the bait. To their credit, they kept it clean; no direct questions, no pressure for insider information. They didn't want to know the messy details. And I didn't offer any. But behind their casual tone was a clear subtext: they were worried, and they wanted to know if this deal was still alive.

Their primary concern was whether this "snag" could be resolved, and how quickly. Timing was critical. The transaction had already been pushed, and the new date was dangerously close to Thanksgiving. The longer things dragged out, the greater the risk of the buyer, Trivest, getting cold feet. Uncertainty is the one thing no deal can afford.

I told them the only thing I could say with a straight face: I hoped that things would resolve on their own. I wanted a path forward as much as they did. But I also knew Dan wasn't going to jump into a new strategy overnight. He'd just been blindsided with a legal shot to the ribs and needed time to catch his breath, assess the damage, and figure out his next move. That meant the earliest possible closing, realistically, was after the holiday.

Meanwhile, Bowles Hollowell Conner & Co. had their own high-wire act to perform. Their role wasn't just to advise or execute; they had to keep Trivest calm and committed. They had to convince the buyer that this delay wasn't the beginning of a collapse, but just a temporary stall. They had to maintain the illusion of stability while quietly scurrying behind the scenes.

In short, they had to do what every great investment banker does in a deal that's gone off-script: manage expectations, suppress panic, and keep the narrative alive.

Everyone was now on edge, working their respective levers to make sure the whole structure didn't come tumbling down.

Chapter Fourteen: Heat in the Kitchen

I didn't have much direct experience with Ariel Gratch, but it didn't take long to realize he wasn't just another New York lawyer riding the clock. Short in stature but burning with intensity, Ariel was a red-haired senior partner at Zellermayer, Gratch, and Jacobs. His reputation preceded him; he was a man who didn't waste words, didn't miss signals, and certainly didn't play games when it came to legal exposure. That said, I found it hard to believe he grasped the extent to which the rot surrounding Dan had festered. The mess with Dan, Alan Jacobs, the TRO, and the lurking threat of "the Problem"—none of it seemed like anything Ariel would tolerate for long once he got a clear picture.

Even after the TRO was served, a strange kind of theater continued between the parties. Term sheets—some involving Dan buying, others involving him selling—kept bouncing back and forth. On the surface, it might've looked like progress, but underneath, everyone knew the clock was ticking and the walls were closing in. The TRO had landed like a thunderclap. And if Ariel hadn't understood the seriousness before, he certainly did now.

On November 20th, Ariel dropped the hammer. In a letter sent to every party involved in the deal, he made his position crystal clear: if by 5:00 p.m. the next day there wasn't a signed, ironclad agreement on the table—one that completely resolved *all* aspects of the Problem—his firm would be walking away from Dan for good. No fanfare or second chances. Zellermayer, Gratch, and Jacobs would cease representing him in any capacity related to the matter.

The timing wasn't an accident either. Ariel knew Alan Jacobs, Dan's primary counsel, had been threading a needle with their firm's ethics, representing Dan on one hand, while claiming to support a broader resolution on the other. That kind of dance might have worked for a while, but Ariel saw the risk. He wasn't about to let the firm catch a bullet for a client spinning out of control. His message was clear: either there was progress, or there was an exit plan—his. The heat was rising on all sides.

Behind the scenes, momentum was shifting. With the TRO now in place, Dan's ability to act as a buyer was crippled. What once felt like a game of options was rapidly becoming a single path: Midland Group buying Dan out and assuming control of Detroit Tool. That was the direction the winds were blowing, and it was becoming hard to ignore.

To make matters worse for Dan, Westinghouse Credit Corp.—the lifeline keeping Detroit Tool on financial life support—had started to lose confidence in him entirely. The flip side was that they were beginning to trust *us*. They respected how we'd moved to contain the chaos. They saw a plan forming, and they liked where it was headed. In fact, they had already called Detroit Tool in default. There was no way they were going to keep pumping money into the company as long as Dan remained part of the picture.

So, while Alan tried to revive some last-ditch $5 million offer from Dan for Midland Group's shares, an offer that was somehow still floating even after the TRO was dead on arrival. My internal valuation pegged Dan's Detroit Tool shares at $8 million. Add a projected $2.5 million from The Shannon Group closing, and we were staring at a potential $10.5 million package. Knock off the $500,000 loan secured against his Detroit Tool Group shares, and we had a clean

$10 million in net value, just enough for a fair buyout and a Midland Group takeover.

By the time Dan was handed the TRO on November 16th, I'd already gone native in the Greensfelder Hemker & Gale offices in downtown St. Louis. As an M&A guy, I was used to setting up camp wherever the action was thickest, and this office had become my ground zero. In New York, the split had always been pretty even: half my time at our 1 Madison Avenue base, the other half shoulder to shoulder with Alan and his crew over at Zellermayer Gratch & Jacobs on Third Avenue. But now the war room was here, and it had a Midwestern accent.

The Greensfelder team welcomed me with open arms; there was no pretension or rolled eyes, and just a sense of a shared purpose and professionalism. Everyone from the receptionists to the partners was helpful, warm, and, most importantly, accustomed to the sort of controlled chaos that came with high-stakes negotiations. While one of the firm's heavyweights, Mr. Gale, was out of town—especially over the fast-approaching Thanksgiving weekend when things kicked into sixth gear—I found myself unofficially occupying his corner office. It was a classic partner's lair: massive windows, dark wood furniture that probably weighed as much as a small car, and the usual trappings of a long, successful legal career—photos with judges and governors, crystal trophies, brass plaques, golf tournament relics. But what caught my eye, something that didn't belong there, were the posters. Three of them, framed and proud, celebrating the iconic *Back to the Future* trilogy. It wasn't exactly your typical law firm wall art, and it felt like Doc Brown had crash-landed in a deposition.

Curiosity, hence, got the better of me. I asked Lisa, Jim Murtha's girlfriend and the indispensable assistant who seemed to know every secret inside those walls, what the story was. She smiled and leaned in close to dish it out. Apparently, back in the day, when someone asked Mr. Gale about his kids, he'd deliver the polished answer you'd expect: "One son is a successful attorney in D.C., the other... well, he is still trying to find his way in California." It was the sort of response that lawyers tell each other over martinis, half joking, and half disappointed.

That "struggling son" turned out to be Bob Gale, the guy who dreamed up *Back to the Future* and penned the screenplay that became a billion-dollar franchise. Once Hollywood came knocking, the story changed fast. The posters went up, and the narrative flipped. Suddenly, Mr. Gale would grin and say, "I've got a son who's a big-time writer and producer in Los Angeles and another who's a lawyer somewhere in Virginia."

The posters reminded me that, sometimes, the one who's off-script ends up writing the best ending.

By the time the dust started to settle, it was clear the TRO hadn't just clipped Dan's wings, it had nailed them to the wall. His flexibility was gone: *poof*. Westinghouse Credit Corp. had pretended they could stomach him. Behind closed doors, their loss of confidence was more like a full-blown eviction notice. Dan had become a liability, not just to the business, but to the very survival of Detroit Tool. On the flip side, the more Westinghouse watched how *we* handled the storm—the calm, the precision, the refusal to take the bait—they started seeing us as something rare: a safe bet.

Eventually, the writing on the wall became a mural; Midland Group would take control of Detroit Tool. And despite the wild complexity of the road ahead, Jim Murtha and I believed we could manage the company. That belief wasn't built on blind optimism; rather, it came from a certain kind of confidence born of fire—*our* fire. Jim had never run anything like this before. Real estate had been his playground, but Detroit Tool, by comparison, was a living organism. It was a creature that breathed steel, cash flow, and unpredictable cycles. But with me on the inside and Dave Wessell continuing to run daily ops in Lebanon, Missouri, we believed it was very doable.

Lee and Ken weren't so sure. They were used to square footage, zoning boards, and tenant improvements, not multi-axis computer numerical controlled machines and inventory turns. The factory floor might as well have been the surface of Mars. Still, despite their nerves, they agreed to move forward. However, it came with one critical condition: I had to stay involved. Thankfully, Dave Wessell, despite his zero background in finance, felt the same way. He knew enough to know what he didn't know, and he knew he'd need help.

I didn't have much else brewing, other than maybe an opportunity to possibly join Bowles Hollowell Conner & Co. once the Problem was finally put to bed. So, over the Thanksgiving weekend, while the rest of America was basting turkeys and yelling at football games, we were neck-deep in negotiations. We hashed out the final terms for Dan's exit and, at the same time, agreed that I'd officially come onboard at Detroit Tool, with the finer points of my comp package to be figured out once the ink dried.

What we were walking into was no longer just a messy corporate divorce; it was a full-blown identity shift. Jim was all vision. The machinery didn't scare him because he didn't intend to run it. He saw possibility, not process. Lee and Ken, however, were wired for operations. They thrived on timelines, budgets, and control, so they were absolutely terrified. Manufacturing was not a spreadsheet; it was a spinning engine with levers they'd never touched. I found myself in the middle: part coach, part shrink, and part translator. I reassured them without over-promising, helped Jim dream without floating off, and tried to keep everyone tethered to reality while embracing something brand new. Because while real estate moves in straight lines, manufacturing is a prism, with spectral colors representing each functional area of the multifaceted operation.

Looking back, one thing still baffles me: why didn't more of my colleagues at Kenmare *care* how the companies they were responsible for actually worked? Not on paper or in a pitch deck. What made them tick? Where were the profits truly made, and where could cracks form? It was as if the mechanics of the businesses were beneath them, some sort of intellectual clutter they, evidently, didn't want to get their hands dirty with the details.

Bill had been right all along. "Stick to what you know best," he told me once. For us, that meant the kind of businesses that weren't glamorous but could kick out serious profits: high know-how, low-tech manufacturing with a strong engineering backbone. Companies that didn't just *make* stuff, they made stuff *well*. They required brains, process, and patience. And we respected that. That's why Bill and I operated differently. From the first flash of due diligence to the final handshake on a sale, we rolled up our sleeves. We spent time with the engineers, shop floor supervisors, and line workers. We walked through operations, tracked margins in real time, and studied the quirks of each market segment like we were learning a new dialect. We *understood* these businesses, not just as investment vehicles, but as living, breathing enterprises. That attention to detail was why our portfolio companies consistently delivered.

Meanwhile, other teams at Kenmare were busy burning money and burying potential. Take the two Kenmare portfolio debacles, starting with Yellow Front. Bankruptcy was practically baked in from the beginning. Then there was Compact Video: same playbook, same disaster. Shiny on the outside, hollow at the core. They didn't bother to learn the business and didn't know how it *really* worked. Just fed it money and prayed for headlines.

And here's where it got personal: Detroit Tool didn't just happen to be raided by Dan; it was *strategically* gutted to cover up the messes left behind by Yellow Front and Compact Video. Money was moved, shuffled, and siphoned. And The Shannon Group? That was the crown jewel. Sold too early, too cheap, all so Dan could clean up his trail. If we had just waited two or three more years to let the business mature, scale, and find its rhythm, there was another $10, maybe $20 million still on the table. Gone.

What should've been a long-term win for Kenmare turned into short-term damage control. Instead of letting the strongest assets carry us forward, Dan used them like sandbags on a sinking ship. It wasn't strategy, it was sheer desperation.

And so, Kenmare Capital, once a promising name in the middle-market private equity world, began its slow descent into *Knightmare Capital*, a place where solid companies were sacrificed to hide bad bets, and where the few of us who actually did the work were left holding the truth like a smoking gun. The tragedy wasn't just what we lost; it was what we could've had if anyone had bothered to care half as much as Bill and I did.

Chapter Fifteen: Sweet Fifteen

Dan had finally caved. After months of posturing, stonewalling, misdirection, and outright denial, he agreed—grudgingly—to surrender his shares in Detroit Tool Group, Inc. This wasn't a moment of enlightenment or some heroic act of self-awareness; it was surrender by necessity. The walls had closed in, the clock had run out, and the legal and financial heat had grown too hot to dodge. The moment he conceded, the gears of resolution finally began to turn in earnest. This was the breakthrough we needed—the hard stop that turned into a green light.

Ariel Gratch, the senior partner at the law firm representing Kenmare Capital and Dan, who had been on the verge of washing his hands of the whole mess, backtracked. With Dan's concession in writing and the path to redemption (both literal and metaphorical) opening up, Ariel allowed his firm to continue representing Dan, for now. Still, trust was thin. This wasn't an embrace; it was a conditional truce. The lead role on Dan's side remained with his lead attorney, Alan Jacobs, who had now become more of a relay runner than a dealmaker. We weren't really negotiating with Dan anymore; we were negotiating with Dan's mouthpiece. And even with Dan boxed into a corner, he was going to claw and scratch through Alan until the very last clause was signed and sealed.

By contrast, our side had momentum and urgency. Thanksgiving weekend wasn't turkey and football for me. While families across the country were napping off pumpkin pie, I was camped out in the Greensfelder Hemker & Gale law offices with Joe Lehrer, working around the clock. The conference room became our war room—notes on walls, computer screens glowing, and endless phone calls and faxes. Our mission: close the deal before the Shannon Group deal falls apart and we lose the $2.5 million lifeline it promised. We were walking a tightrope with no safety net.

Of that $2.5 million, $2 million was set to land in Detroit Tool's bank account in Lebanon, Missouri—oxygen for a company on the verge of financial life support without the resumption of support by Westinghouse Credit Corp. The remaining $500,000 was earmarked to pay off Southside National Bank, which still held the lien on Dan's Detroit Tool Group shares. Missed that window, and everything unraveled—our deal, our leverage, and the company's chance of survival.

Meanwhile, on a more pleasant note, a surprising friendship had started to blossom. Jim and his girlfriend Lisa had become fast friends with Lynn and me. In fact, they joined us for Thanksgiving dinner—wine, laughter, and warm conversation, just hours before I disappeared into the legal trenches. It was a strange juxtaposition: comfort and chaos, connection and conflict, all taking place within a 24-hour span.

The stakes were sky-high, and as we entered the final phase of documentation—redlining language, debating warranties, carving out reps, we weren't just cleaning up a mess, we were laying the foundation for a new chapter, one built not on illusion, but on transparency, discipline, and actual operational know-how.

This is a summary of the final documentation of the resolution to the Problem:

Stock Purchase Agreement and Related Documents

- **Accounting of Transferred Funds**: Daniel J. Sullivan ("DJS") and Kenmare Capital Corp.

("KCC") shall provide a full accounting of all cash and property of Detroit Tool Group, Inc. ("DTG") and its subsidiaries that were transferred to, or for the benefit of, KCC, DJS, and their affiliates. This accounting is to be verified by DTG's independent accountants and must be acceptable in both form and computation to Westinghouse Credit Corporation ("WCC"). The total sum identified through this process, plus interest at an annual rate of 10%, minus any amounts already returned to DTG, will be defined as the "Transferred Funds."

- **Transfer of Purchased Stock:** DJS agrees to sell and transfer to DTG 30,900 shares of DTG Common Stock, par value $0.01 per share (the "Purchased Stock"), which represents all equity interests owned by DJS, KCC, or their affiliates. This block constitutes 51.5% of DTG's outstanding common stock (prior to dilution from WCC's 15,000-share warrant). At closing, these shares shall be transferred free and clear of all liens, claims, and encumbrances.

- **Purchase Price and Offset:** The agreed-upon purchase price for the Purchased Stock is $8 million. This amount will be satisfied through a reduction of DTG's receivable related to the Transferred Funds as of the Closing. DTG will execute appropriate documentation acknowledging this offset against indebtedness.

- **Payment of Remaining Transferred Funds:** Any remaining balance of the Transferred Funds, after deducting the $8 million purchase price, shall be paid directly to DTG at Closing.

- **Comprehensive Release from Liability:** Upon Closing, DTG, David Wessell, President of the Detroit Tool operating companies in Lebanon, Missouri, Midland Detroit Tool Group ("Midland"), DTG's board of directors, and WCC will issue a full release of liability to DJS, KCC, their affiliates, Andrew Mayer, and their respective legal and professional representatives in connection with the Transferred Funds. DJS and KCC warrant that all such funds and assets have been fully disclosed and accounted for.

- **Resignation and Termination of Prior Agreements:** DJS and Andrew Mayer will resign from all officer and director positions within DTG and its subsidiaries. In addition, DJS, KCC, and their affiliates will terminate any prior agreements with DTG—including, but not limited to, management, consulting, and employment agreements—and will release DTG, its officers, and directors from any claims or liabilities relating to the Transferred Funds.

- **Mutual Release of Liability:** DJS, KCC, and Andrew Mayer will issue a full release to WCC and its employees and assets from any and all liabilities.
- **Termination of Shareholder Agreements:** All existing agreements among DJS and DTG shareholders—including any Shareholder Agreements and Voting Trusts—will be terminated in full.
- **Resale Agreement Contingency:** At Closing, DTG and DJS will enter into a **Resale Agreement** stipulating that, if within three years from the Closing date, all or part of DTG's stock, its subsidiaries, or a substantial portion of their assets is sold, a computation of net proceeds (after transaction costs) will be made. If DJS had been entitled to an amount greater than $8 million based on his pre-sale ownership percentage, DTG will pay DJS 50% of the excess. Notably, the $8 million benchmark will increase by any additional capital contributed by Midland. *(This clause, true to Dan's "you don't get what you don't ask for" philosophy, was the only concession I made during final negotiations, though not without shortening the fuse.)*

- **Waiver of Defaults by WCC:** Subject to WCC's satisfaction with the final documentation, WCC will waive all existing Events of Default under the Loan and Security Agreement, all related agreements, and the Warrants, specifically those triggered by the diversion of DTG's corporate assets in the amount of the Transferred Funds.

The Closing took place over two long days behind the glass walls of the Greensfelder Hemker & Gale office in St. Louis. It wasn't a celebration; it was a silent execution. The end of an era. Dan flew in from New York under two strict conditions: he would be the first to sign the documents, and I would not be in the room. That was fine with me. He had already lost. Watching him ink the paper would've only added salt to the wound, and I had no interest in gloating. I was there to finish the job, not savor it.

I signed everything the next day. By then, the accountants had confirmed three critical things: the Transferred Funds had been accounted for, the Southside National Bank loan had been fully paid, and the wire transfer, just over $2 million, had hit Commerce Bank in Lebanon, Missouri. It was official. The Problem was no longer a problem.

Needless to say, I never spoke to Dan again. No calls, letters, and no sideways jabs through mutual contacts.

Nothing. Zilch. He was checkmated in a game of financial chess, and and that it was me who moved the final piece would probably haunt him for the rest of his life. He didn't lose the company; he got outplayed. That's a tough pill to swallow, especially for someone like Dan.

About a year after I was let go, a letter arrived. It was from Bill. He had retired shortly after I left. I sensed the tone to be more reflective, almost apologetic. He admitted that, with distance and time, he could finally see it clearly: I'd done the right thing. That letter wasn't closure, but it was a kind of truth. A small nod across the battlefield, long after the smoke had cleared.

Then came the Lucite tombstone from Bowles Hollowell Conner & Co.—one of those slick, transparent deal trophies they send out when the ink dries on a major transaction. This one marked the sale of The Shannon Group to Trivest. I didn't work there anymore, but they knew who built it, who steered it, and who got it out clean. That tombstone sat on my shelf like a grinning ghost. It was proof that I didn't just survive the storm, I captained the damn ship through it.

In May 1992, I ran into Bob Silva at the Marriott in San Diego. He looked worn, but light as a feather. He told me that he had left Kenmare "way too late," with the same half-smile guys wear when they've been burned but weren't bitter. By late '91, the firm had collapsed into itself like a dying star. Everyone but Dan got roasted, and Bob finally understood, and so did Bill. Sometimes you have to burn bridges just to keep warm.

I invited Bob to watch the America's Cup from the Commodore's boat, and he decided to stay an extra day to join us. Jim Murtha's friend had rotated into the Commodore's office that year—pure dumb luck. Fred showed up with his old 40-footer that barely floated, but the beer was cold, the wind was good, and for one long afternoon, the war was far behind us.

After helping Midland steady the Detroit Tool ship for a little over a year, I stepped away; I'd done what needed to be done. The mess had been cleaned up, the books balanced, the ghosts more or less buried. I was ready to move on. Midland, always more at home in the bricks-and-mortar comfort of real estate, never fully warmed to the idea of managing a gritty industrial operation. Within two years of taking the wheel, they sold 100% of their stake in Detroit Tool to a St. Louis-based investment group. That group wasted no time; they polished it up a little more and took the company public not long after. Another notch in someone's belt. Another company... spun and sold.

Dan abandoned Steve Trampe. He fled to Europe, leaving him alone and saddled with over $40 million in bank guarantees related to their real estate ventures in St Louis. Without any support whatsoever from Dan, it took Steve over 10 years to resolve them. Once on his own, he built a name for himself as a serious player in the St. Louis real estate game. No noise, no drama—just smart deals and solid dirt under his feet.

A few years later, I reached out to Bill. Time softens things, or maybe it just wears them down. In 1998, the Page family packed up and made a visit to Osterville on Cape Cod to visit Bill Laverty, my incredible mentor at Kenmare Capital, and his wife, Margaret. Our son, William E. Page, was seven years old at the time, the same age I was when I first started visiting my dad from time to time at his office in lower Manhattan. That day, he got to meet William J. Laverty. Old Bill. The man who once handed me both opportunity and fire, sometimes in the same sentence. It felt right, even necessary.

The final chapter with Kenmare didn't come with fanfare. A few years after that visit, Lynn and I got a handwritten note from Margaret: Bill had passed away a couple of weeks earlier. Old age, she said. He went quietly and in a dignified way, just like he had been his whole life.

Epilogue

I've always believed that everything happens for a reason, and that if you do the right thing, even when it's hard, life eventually sorts itself out. Things may not have gone down exactly the way I envisioned, but looking back now, I wouldn't trade my years at Kenmare for anything. Not for a safer role, a more stable path, or a bigger paycheck. That chapter of my life was too rich, too full of sharp turns, wild lessons, and unforgettable characters, to ever regret.

Working at Kenmare was like being dropped into the middle of a live wire deal almost every day. The people I met, the places I flew to, the tightrope negotiations, late nights out, the midnight calls, and the long games and short fuses, like a trial by fire. And the skills I built, like how to read a room, close a deal, stay calm in chaos, and outthink the guy who thinks he's the one outthinking you, you don't learn that sitting in a cubicle for 40 hours a week.

And the irony is that all of that training set me up perfectly for life *after* Kenmare. From cleaning up the Problem, to eventually building and operating my own portfolio of small, hands-on, know-how-over-flash manufacturing businesses. I even got to help other people turn around companies as a consultant, using the same toolkit I picked up back in those Kenmare war rooms. Best of all, I got to do it from St. Louis, and not from some airport lounge somewhere in North America or Europe over 300 days a year. I was home with Lynn, raising William. Being there for the real stuff. And that was the real win for me. That was the whole point.

Now, decades later, we're still in the same house where Lynn and I were married — inside the white picket fence that once held a sandbox and a rope swing, and now frames a serene and happy life. William has grown up, launched, married, and is living just outside London, making his own way in the world. And us? We're good. Life worked out, it really did.

But every so often, I think about Dan. Not necessarily with anger, but more with curiosity. I wonder what it'd be like to run into him now — maybe in an airport, walking through a concourse, or waiting at a gate, two lives bumping into the past for a moment. I seem to have a strange knack for bumping into people I haven't seen in decades; someone from a deal, a dorm, or a different era, right there by the moving walkway.

So, what would it be with Dan? After all the years, would he give me a grin or a scowl? A nod or just walk on by?

It wouldn't be like Andy's call that night, the one where he said, simply, *you were good*. No, Dan wouldn't say that. That wasn't his style. But that's okay, since some truths don't need to be spoken to be known.

www.ingramcontent.com/pod-product-compliance
Lightning Source LLC
LaVergne TN
LVHW050816061126
851857LV00012B/827
* 9 7 9 8 2 9 5 4 1 5 0 5 0 *